Mastering Bash Scripting
From Basics to Expert Proficiency

Contents

Introduction

Bash scripting is a vital skill for any system administrator, developer, or IT professional. It is a powerful language that allows users to automate tasks, streamline workflows, and enhance productivity. This book, "Mastering Bash Scripting: From Basics to Expert Proficiency," aims to provide a comprehensive guide to Bash scripting, from fundamental concepts to advanced techniques.

Bourne Again Shell, or Bash, is a command language that provides a user interface for the Unix/Linux operating system. It is an interactive command language, as well as a scripting language, and is ubiquitous in the world of Unix-like operating systems. Learning Bash scripting not only helps in automating repetitive tasks but also in understanding the underlying mechanisms of the Unix/Linux systems, making users more proficient and competent.

This book is meticulously curated to cater to both beginners who are just stepping into the world of Bash scripting and experienced users looking to refine their skills. Each chapter builds upon the previous one, ensuring a solid foundation while progressively introducing more complex topics.

In the initial chapters, readers will be introduced to the essentials of Bash scripting, including the history and evolution of Bash, basic command line usage, and executing scripts. Setting up the environment correctly is crucial for scripting, and thus, detailed instructions on configuring your shell environment, installing necessary tools, and customizing your terminal are provided.

Understanding the core concepts, such as Bash syntax, command options, and variables, is fundamental. Therefore, chapters dedicated to these topics will provide in-depth explanations and examples. Control structures, such as loops and conditional statements, are pivotal in creating more dynamic and functional scripts, and this book covers these extensively.

Functions are a critical component in any programming language, and Bash is no exception. Readers will learn how to define, call, and use functions effectively, making scripts modular and reusable. Input and output handling, a frequently encountered task in scripting, is elucidated with practical examples.

Working with files and directories is an everyday task for Bash users. This book delves into various file operations, permission management, and automation of file management tasks. Advanced scripting techniques are covered in detail, including regular expressions, text manipulation, concurrent execution, and secure scripting practices.

Debugging and testing Bash scripts are essential for ensuring reliability and efficiency. The final chapters of this book provide methodologies for debugging, using testing tools, and implementing best practices for maintaining high-quality scripts.

In summary, "Mastering Bash Scripting: From Basics to Expert Proficiency" is designed to be an authoritative resource that equips readers with the knowledge and skills necessary to excel in Bash scripting. Whether the goal is to automate tasks, enhance productivity, or gain a deeper understanding of Unix/Linux systems, this book serves as an indispensable guide for mastering Bash scripting.

Chapter 1

Introduction to Bash Scripting

This chapter provides a comprehensive overview of Bash scripting, covering its definition, historical background, and key reasons for learning it. It introduces readers to basic command line usage and the terminal, guiding them through the creation and execution of their first Bash script. Additionally, it explores common applications of Bash scripting and offers an overview of the scripting language, concluding with resources for further learning and reading.

1.1 What is Bash?

Bash, which stands for Bourne Again SHell, is a Unix shell and command language written by Brian Fox for the GNU Project as a free software replacement for the Bourne shell ($/\mathrm{bin}/\mathrm{sh}$). Bash is an sh-compatible shell that incorporates useful features from the Korn shell (ksh) and the C shell (csh). It was first released in 1989 and has since become one of the most widely used shells for both interactive and scripting purposes.

As a command language interpreter, Bash provides a user interface for the Unix operating system. Upon invocation, Bash reads and executes commands from standard input or a file. It operates within the shell environment, maintaining the state of shell variables and functions, and managing the execution of foreground and background jobs.

Key features of Bash include command-line editing, key bindings, unlimited command history, shell scripting capabilities, and various built-in commands. These features make Bash a powerful and versatile tool for system administrators, programmers, and power users alike.

- **Command-line Editing:** Allows users to edit the command line text before execution. This feature supports Emacs and Vi editing modes, providing flexibility based on user preference.
- **Key Bindings:** Customize the keyboard shortcuts for various shell functions, allowing efficient and personalized command execution.
- **Unlimited Command History:** Stores previously executed commands in a history file, enabling users to recall and reuse prior commands with ease.
- **Shell Scripting Capabilities:** Automates repetitive tasks and complex workflows by writing scripts that consist of multiple commands executed in sequence.
- **Built-in Commands:** A set of internal commands that are executed directly within the shell without invoking separate binaries. Examples include cd, echo, and export.

Bash scripts are typically text files containing a series of commands that can be executed by the Bash shell. These scripts start with a shebang (#!/bin/bash) line at the top, indicating that the script should be run using the Bash interpreter. The following example demonstrates a simple Bash script:

```
#!/bin/bash
# This is a simple Bash script

echo "Hello, World!"
```

When executed, this script produces the following output:

```
Hello, World!
```

One of the strengths of Bash is its compatibility with various Unix-based systems, making it a portable and reliable choice for cross-platform scripting. It is included by default in many Unix-like operating systems, including Linux distributions and macOS. This widespread availability ensures that scripts written for Bash will run on a diverse range of systems without requiring modifications.

The syntax of Bash is derived from the Bourne shell, providing a fundamental structure for command execution, variable handling, and control flow constructs such as loops and conditionals. Bash supports features like command substitution, process substitution, and arithmetic expansion, which enhance its functionality and flexibility.

```
# Example of variable handling and arithmetic expansion in Bash
#!/bin/bash
# Define variables
a=5
b=10

# Perform arithmetic operation
(( sum = a + b ))

# Output result
echo "The sum of a and b is: $sum"
```

The preceding script defines two variables, a and b, assigns them values, performs an arithmetic operation to calculate their sum, and outputs the result. The script produces the following result:

```
The sum of a and b is: 15
```

Bash provides a robust set of built-in commands and functions, enabling users to perform a wide range of tasks directly within the shell. These include file and directory manipulation, text processing, and system administration. Examples of commonly used built-in commands are as follows:

```
# Example of built-in commands in Bash
#!/bin/bash

# Make a new directory
mkdir new_directory

# Change to the new directory
cd new_directory

# Create a new file
touch new_file.txt

# Write to the file
echo "This is a new file." > new_file.txt

# Display the contents of the file
cat new_file.txt
```

```
# Delete the file
rm new_file.txt

# Go back to the previous directory
cd ..
```

When executed, the script will create a new directory called new_directory, navigate into it, create a new file called new_file.txt, write a line of text into the file, display the file's contents, and finally delete the file and return to the previous directory.

Understanding and using Bash effectively includes mastering its command syntax, built-in functions, and scripting capabilities. Bash provides an interactive environment and a powerful scripting tool, making it indispensable for users requiring automation and efficiency in managing Unix-based systems.

1.2 History and Evolution of Bash

The Bourne Again Shell, commonly known as Bash, is a Unix shell and command language written by Brian Fox for the GNU Project as a free software replacement for the Bourne Shell (sh). First released in 1989, Bash has become the default shell on many Linux distributions and a de facto standard for shell scripting today.

Bash's lineage can be traced back to the original Unix shell, known as the Thompson shell, developed by Ken Thompson. This initial shell lacked several features we now consider fundamental; however, it paved the way for the development of more advanced shells, including the Bourne Shell.

The Bourne Shell (sh), developed by Stephen Bourne at AT&T Bell Labs and released in 1979, introduced many features that became staples in modern shell programming, such as control flow structures (e.g., if...then...else, for, while), environment variables, and user-defined functions. While powerful, the Bourne Shell had limitations, particularly in interactive use.

In response to the need for more robust interactive features, the **C Shell (csh)** was developed by Bill Joy in the late 1970s at UC Berkeley. csh introduced history substitution, aliasing, and improved interactive capabilities. However, its scripting syntax was less intuitive than sh.

During this time, variations of shells continued to evolve:

- **Korn Shell (ksh)**: Developed by David Korn in the early 1980s, it combined features from the Bourne Shell and the C Shell while adding new features like associative arrays, improved string handling, and built-in arithmetic operations.
- **Bourne-Again Shell (Bash)**: Conceived as part of the GNU Project, the need for a free shell that incorporated the best features of both sh and csh, with added enhancements, led to the creation of Bash.

Bash incorporated:

- Command-line editing via Emacs and Vi modes.
- Command history, facilitating the recall and editing of previous commands.
- Job control, allowing the management of background and foreground processes.
- Improved scripting capabilities over sh, including array variables and additional scripting syntactic sugar.

Below is a timeline summarizing the evolution of major Unix Shells that influenced Bash:

Year	Shell	Developer
1971	sh	Ken Thompson
1979	sh	Stephen Bourne
Late 1970s	csh	Bill Joy
Early 1980s	ksh	David Korn
1989	Bash	Brian Fox (for GNU Project)

Bash has not remained static since its initial release. Subsequent updates have introduced numerous features and improvements. Significant versions include:

- **Bash 1.x** (June 1989): Initial public release integrating features from sh, csh, and ksh.
- **Bash 2.x** (December 1996): Enhanced array support, command substitution improvements, and additional scripting features.

- **Bash 3.x** (July 2004): Introduced [[...]] for improved conditional test expressions, arithmetic for loops, augmented arrays, and other scripting enhancements.
- **Bash 4.x** (February 2009): Added associative arrays, coproc for concurrent processing, and the ** and ++ arithmetic operators.
- **Bash 5.x** (January 2019): Introduced new variable modifiers, including nameref, revamped random number generation, and performance improvements.

Bash continues to evolve with contributions from numerous developers and its use across various platforms, including non-Unix systems. As of today, Bash has become an essential tool for system administrators, developers, and power users due to its powerful scripting capabilities and flexibility in automating tasks. The collaboration and continuous enhancements ensure it remains relevant and robust for modern computing needs.

1.3 Why Learn Bash Scripting?

Bash scripting has become an indispensable skill for system administrators, developers, and anyone working in a Unix-like environment. Its utility is multifaceted, providing solutions tailored to a variety of computational and administrative problems. Learning Bash scripting not only enhances efficiency but also deepens one's understanding of the command line interface.

Automation of Repetitive Tasks: One of the primary reasons to learn Bash scripting is its ability to automate repetitive tasks. For instance, consider the need to rename a batch of files systematically. Manually renaming each file is time-consuming and prone to error. Bash scripts can automate this process with precision and speed. Here is an example script to rename all .txt files to .text files in a directory:

```
#!/bin/bash

for file in *.txt; do
  mv "$file" "${file%.txt}.text"
done
```

System Administration: Effective system administration frequently requires the execution of repetitive tasks such as monitoring system performance, managing disk space, and automating backups. Bash scripting streamlines these processes. An example script to monitor disk space and send an alert if usage exceeds a specified threshold might look as follows:

```
#!/bin/bash

THRESHOLD=80
USAGE=$(df / | grep / | awk '{ print $5 }' | sed 's/%//g')

if [ $USAGE -gt $THRESHOLD ]; then
  echo "Disk space critically low. Usage is at ${USAGE}%." | mail -s "Disk Space Alert
        " user@example.com
fi
```

Handling Text and Data Files: Bash scripting excels at manipulating text and data files. Scripts can be used to extract, process, and transform data efficiently. When working with log files or data dumps, Bash provides tools like grep, awk, and sed to manipulate text. For example, a script to extract lines matching a specific pattern from a log file might use:

```
#!/bin/bash

grep 'ERROR' /var/log/syslog > error_log.txt
```

Integration with Other Tools: Bash scripts can seamlessly integrate with other command-line tools and software. This enables the creation of powerful toolchains for complex workflows. For example, combining curl for fetching web content, jq for parsing JSON, and Bash scripting, one can easily automate interactions with web APIs:

```
#!/bin/bash

API_URL="https://api.example.com/data"
RESPONSE=$(curl -s $API_URL)
VALUE=$(echo $RESPONSE | jq '.key')

echo "The value of 'key' is $VALUE"
```

Task Scheduling: The ability to schedule tasks using cron jobs amplifies the power of Bash scripting. Scheduling scripts to run at specific intervals can automate maintenance and monitoring tasks with little oversight. A cron job to run a backup script daily at midnight can be set up as follows:

```
0 0 * * * /path/to/backup_script.sh
```

Cross-Platform Compatibility: Bash is available on virtually all Unix-like operating systems, including Linux and macOS. Scripts written in Bash can be executed across these platforms without modification, ensuring broad applicability and ease of sharing.

Learning Curve and Readability: The syntax of Bash is relatively straightforward, making it accessible even to beginners. Additionally, the readability of Bash scripts is enhanced by using comments and clear variable names. An illustrative script demonstrating good practices in this regard is:

```
#!/bin/bash

# This script generates a report of disk usage
OUTPUT="/var/log/disk_usage_report.txt"
THRESHOLD=85

# Generate disk usage report
df -h > $OUTPUT

# Check if any partition exceeds the threshold
while read line; do
  USAGE=$(echo $line | awk '{ print $5 }' | sed 's/%//g')
  if [ $USAGE -ge $THRESHOLD ]; then
    echo "Warning: Partition exceeds threshold" >> $OUTPUT
  fi
done < <(tail -n +2 $OUTPUT)
```

Bash scripting promotes good coding practices and problem-solving skills. Mastering Bash can act as a gateway to learning other programming languages and scripting utilities, markedly enhancing one's computational toolkit. Functionality, flexibility, and the ability to influence and automate system behaviors are strong motivations for gaining proficiency in Bash scripting.

1.4 Basic Command Line Usage

Understanding basic command line usage is fundamental for anyone beginning with Bash scripting. The command line interface (CLI) is a text-based interface used to interact with the operating system, allowing for direct communication with the computer's core functionalities through text commands.

To open a terminal on a Unix-like operating system, one typically searches for the terminal application in the system's application menu. Once opened, a prompt is displayed, usually ending with a dollar sign ($), indicating readiness to accept commands.

Basic command structure:

```
command [options] [arguments]
```

In this structure, command is the instruction you want the system to execute. Options modify the behavior of the command, and arguments specify the object upon which the command should act.

- **pwd:** Prints the current working directory.

```
pwd
```

/home/user

- **ls:** Lists files and directories in the current directory.

```
ls
```

Documents Downloads Music Pictures Videos

- **cd:** Changes the current directory.

```
cd Documents
```

user@machine:~/Documents$

- **mkdir:** Creates a new directory.

```
mkdir new_directory
```

user@machine:~/Documents$

- **rmdir:** Removes an empty directory.

```
rmdir new_directory
```

user@machine:~/Documents$

- **rm:** Removes a file or directory. Use -r to remove directories and their contents recursively.

```
rm file.txt
```

user@machine:~/Documents$

Commands may have various options that modify their behavior. For instance, the ls command can be used with the -l option to provide a detailed listing, displaying permissions, number of links, owner, group, size, and time of last modification.

```
ls -l
```

```
total 0
drwxrwxr-x 2 user user 4096 Jan 1 12:00 Documents
drwxrwxr-x 2 user user 4096 Feb 1 12:00 Downloads
drwxrwxr-x 2 user user 4096 Mar 1 12:00 Music
drwxrwxr-x 2 user user 4096 Apr 1 12:00 Pictures
drwxrwxr-x 2 user user 4096 May 1 12:00 Videos
```

Options can often be combined. For instance, ls -la provides a detailed listing of all files, including hidden files (those starting with a dot).

Understanding file permissions is crucial for managing and scripting within the Bash environment. File permissions, displayed by ls -l, show who can read, write, or execute a file or directory:

```
-rw-r--r-- 1 user user 0 Jan 1 12:00 file.txt
```

Permissions are set in three groups:

- **The owner (user)**
- **The group**
- **Others**

The output -rw-r–r– is broken down as follows:

- The first character, -, indicates a regular file. (Directory is d, link is l.)
- The next three characters, rw-, refer to the permissions for the user: read and write.
- The following three, r–, refer to the permissions for the group: read only.
- The last three, r–, are for others: read only.

Permissions can be changed using the chmod command. If you wish to make a file executable:

```
chmod +x script.sh
```

To change the ownership of a file, use the chown command:

```
chown user:group file.txt
```

Command chaining allows for executing multiple commands in sequence. This is managed using operators such as semicolon (;), double ampersand (&&), and double pipe (||):

- command1 ; command2: Executes command1, then command2, regardless of success or failure of command1.
- command1 && command2: Executes command1, and if it succeeds, executes command2.
- command1 || command2: Executes command1, and if it fails, executes command2.

Piping (|) is used to pass the output of one command as input to another. For example, to list directory contents and view it page by page:

```
ls -l | less
```

Another essential concept is input/output redirection. This modifies the default behavior of standard input, output, and error:

- command > file: Redirects standard output to a file (overwriting if it exists).
- command » file: Redirects standard output to a file (appending to it if it exists).
- command 2> file: Redirects standard error to a file.
- command < file: Takes standard input from a file.

Combining these basic command line operations with proper understanding and practice forms the foundation of effective Bash scripting. This basis equips learners to futuristically build more complex scripts efficiently.

1.5 Understanding the Terminal

The terminal, also known as the command line interface (CLI) or shell, is a powerful tool that allows users to interact directly with the operating system. Unlike graphical user interfaces (GUIs), the terminal provides a text-based environment where commands are executed to perform specific tasks. Understanding the terminal is crucial for mastering Bash scripting, as it lays the foundation for more advanced scripting techniques.

Terminal Basics

The terminal operates in a read-evaluate-print loop (REPL), where it reads a command from the user, evaluates (executes) it, prints the output, and then waits for the next command. Each command entered in the terminal consists of a command itself and possibly additional arguments or options.

For example, consider the following command:

```
$ ls -l /home/user
```

In this command:

- ls is the command.
- -l is an option modifying the behavior of the command.
- /home/user is an argument specifying the location to list.

Prompt

The terminal prompt indicates that the terminal is ready to receive commands. It usually consists of the username, hostname, and current working directory, followed by a special character (commonly $ for standard users and # for the root user). For instance:

user@hostname:~$

This prompt shows that the user is in the home directory (denoted by ~).

Navigating the Filesystem

Commands like cd, pwd, ls, and others are fundamental for navigating the filesystem.

- cd: Changes the current directory. For example:

```
$ cd /var/log
```

- pwd: Prints the working directory.

```
$ pwd
/var/log
```

- ls: Lists directory contents.

```
$ ls
syslog kern.log
```

File and Directory Operations

File and directory operations form the core of terminal usage. Below are some essential commands for manipulating files and directories:

- cp: Copies files or directories.

```
$ cp file1.txt /tmp/
```

- mv: Moves or renames files or directories.

```
$ mv file1.txt /home/user/docs/
```

- rm: Removes files or directories.

```
$ rm file1.txt
```

- mkdir: Creates a new directory.

```
$ mkdir new_directory
```

Text Editors

Editing scripts directly in the terminal requires proficiency in terminal-based text editors. Common text editors include nano, vim, and emacs. Here, we provide a simple example using nano:

```
$ nano script.sh
```

This command opens the file script.sh in the nano editor. Basic commands in nano include:

- Ctrl+O: Write (save) the file.
- Ctrl+X: Exit the editor.
- Ctrl+K: Cut a line of text.
- Ctrl+U: Uncut (paste) the line of text.

Understanding Permissions

File permissions are crucial in the terminal environment, determining who can read, write, or execute a file. The ls -l command displays permissions in the form of a string like -rwxr-xr-x. The first character indicates if it is a directory (d) or a file (-). The next nine characters are divided into three groups of three, representing the permissions for the owner, group, and others respectively.

```
-rwxr-xr-x 1 user group 4096 Jan 1 12:34 script.sh
```

To change permissions, one uses the chmod command. For example, to make the script.sh executable by the owner:

```
$ chmod u+x script.sh
```

Environment Variables

Environment variables store configuration settings and preferences. Common environment variables include HOME, PATH, and USER. You can view environment variables using the echo command:

```
$ echo $HOME
/home/user
```

Setting an environment variable can be done as follows:

```
$ export MY_VAR=HelloWorld
```

Command History and Re-execution

The terminal maintains a history of commands executed. You can navigate this history using the Up and Down arrow keys. The history command displays recently executed commands:

```
$ history
1 ls
2 cd /var/log
3 pwd
```

To re-execute a specific command from history, use the exclamation mark (!) followed by the command number:

```
$ !2 # This runs 'cd /var/log' again
```

Wildcards and Pattern Matching

Wildcards are essential for matching file names and patterns. Common wildcards include:

- *: Matches any number of characters.
- ?: Matches a single character.
- [range]: Matches any character within the specified range.

For example, to list all text files in a directory:

```
$ ls *.txt
```

Understanding the terminal forms the backbone of efficient and effective Bash scripting. It provides a powerful interface for interacting with the operating system, performing various tasks, and ultimately scripting these tasks to automate processes. Mastery of the terminal commands and conventions is paramount in advancing further into Bash scripting proficiency.

1.6 The First Bash Script

Creating your first Bash script involves several fundamental steps, from writing the script to making it executable, and finally running it. This section provides detailed instructions and explanations for each of these steps to ensure a clear understanding.

First, open a text editor of your choice, such as nano, vim, or gedit. For simplicity, we will use nano here.

To create a new file in nano, open the terminal and type:

```
nano first_script.sh
```

This command will open a new file named first_script.sh in the nano editor. The .sh extension is commonly used for Bash scripts.

In the newly opened nano editor, write the following lines:

```
#!/bin/bash
# This is our first Bash script

echo "Hello, World!"
```

Let's break down the components of this script:

- #!/bin/bash: This is known as the shebang line. It tells the system that the script should be run using the Bash shell located at /bin/bash.
- # This is our first Bash script: Lines starting with # are comments. Comments are ignored by the Bash interpreter and are used to provide explanations or notes for human readers.
- echo "Hello, World!": The echo command outputs the text "Hello, World!" to the terminal.

After writing the script, save the file by pressing CTRL+O, then press Enter. Exit nano by pressing CTRL+X.

To execute the script, it must be made executable. In the terminal, type:

```
chmod +x first_script.sh
```

This command changes the file permissions, making it executable. The chmod command modifies file permissions, and +x adds the execute permission.

Now, to run the script, type:

```
./first_script.sh
```

The ./ indicates that the script should be run from the current directory. The expected output in the terminal should be:

```
Hello, World!
```

This process demonstrates the essential steps to create, write, save, and execute a simple Bash script. Understanding these basics forms the foundation for more advanced scripting.

Let's delve deeper into some common issues and their troubleshooting:

1. Permission Denied Error:

If you see a Permission denied error, it means that the script does not have execute permissions. Ensure that you have run the chmod +x first_script.sh command to correct this.

2. Command Not Found Error:

If you encounter a command not found error, first check the script for typos. If the script is correct, make sure the #!/bin/bash shebang line points to the correct path of the Bash shell. You can verify the path with the which bash command. Adjust the shebang line accordingly if the path is different.

3. Unexpected Output:

If the script executes but the output is not as expected, review the script for logical errors in commands or syntax. Each command should be on a separate line, and all comment lines must start with #.

Practice by modifying the script to include more echo statements or simple commands. For example, add another line:

```
echo "Welcome to Bash scripting!"
```

Update the script:

```
#!/bin/bash
# This is our first Bash script

echo "Hello, World!"
echo "Welcome to Bash scripting!"
```

Save the script and run it again. The expected output should now be:

```
Hello, World!
Welcome to Bash Scripting!
```

These exercises reinforce the core concepts of Bash scripting, enabling you to develop more complex scripts with confidence.

1.7 Executing Bash Scripts

Executing a Bash script involves running the code contained within the script file, typically a text file with a .sh extension, using the Bash shell interpreter. This process can be achieved through various methods depending on the user's environment and preferences. This section will outline these methods in detail, considering different scenarios and illustrating examples to reinforce understanding.

Assume that a simple script named example.sh contains the following content:

```
#!/bin/bash

echo "Hello, World!"
```

The above script uses the echo command to print "Hello, World!" to the terminal.

1. Using the Bash Command

The most direct way to execute a script is by calling the Bash interpreter explicitly through the command line:

```
$ bash example.sh
```

In this approach, bash is the command that invokes the Bash interpreter, and example.sh is the name of the script file.

```
Hello, World!
```

2. Making the Script Executable

Another method involves modifying the script file to make it executable. This requires altering the file permissions to include execution (x) permissions using the chmod command:

```
$ chmod +x example.sh
```

After changing the permissions, the script can be executed directly by invoking its filename preceded by a relative or absolute path:

```
$ ./example.sh
```

```
Hello, World!
```

The prefix ./ specifies the current directory as the location of the executable script. This avoids potential ambiguities if there are other executables with the same name in the system's PATH.

3. Using sh Command

Another standard way to execute Bash scripts, especially on systems where Bash might not be the default shell, is by using the sh command:

```
$ sh example.sh
```

However, it is crucial to note that the sh command invokes the default shell, which might not always be Bash. For Bash-specific features, using bash is recommended.

4. From Within Another Script

Scripts can also be executed from within other scripts. Consider another script named launcher.sh, which calls example.sh:

```
#!/bin/bash

./example.sh
```

Ensure that example.sh has execution permissions if it is invoked in this manner. Running launcher.sh will result in:

```
$ bash launcher.sh
```

```
Hello, World!
```

5. Using Source or Dot Command

The source command (or its shorthand .) executes a script in the current shell context rather than spawning a subshell:

```
$ source example.sh
# or
$ . example.sh
```

Using this method, any variables or functions defined in the script persist in the calling shell session, which is crucial for scripts that modify the shell environment. To illustrate:

```
#!/bin/bash

MYVAR="Hello from the script"
```

Executing the above script using source:

```
$ source example.sh
$ echo $MYVAR
```

```
Hello from the script
```

This contrasts with executing the script normally, where MYVAR would not be accessible in the current shell session after the script execution completes.

6. Conditional Execution

Bash also permits the conditional execution of scripts, typically within shell logic structures. For example, executing a script if a specific condition is met:

```
if [ -f example.sh ]; then
  ./example.sh
fi
```

This snippet checks if example.sh exists before execution.

7. Environment Considerations

When executing scripts, it is crucial to be aware of the environment context, including environment variables and the shell's path settings. For example:

```
$ PATH="/custom/path:$PATH" ./example.sh
```

This command temporarily modifies the PATH environment variable for the script execution session.

Through these examples, the process of executing Bash scripts can adapt to varied situations. Understanding these methods ensures robust and versatile script execution aligned with specific requirements and user environments.

1.8 Common Uses of Bash Scripting

Bash scripting serves a multitude of purposes across various domains, owing to its versatility and powerful capabilities in automating repetitive tasks. Here, we will discuss some of the most common applications and illustrate how they can streamline processes effectively.

1. Automating Routine Tasks

Bash scripts are often employed to automate tasks that would be tedious and time-consuming if performed manually. Examples include:

- Backing up files and directories at regular intervals.
- Renaming, moving, or deleting large numbers of files based on specific criteria.
- Synchronizing files across directories or systems using tools like rsync.
- Monitoring system performance and resource usage.

For instance, consider a script that automates the backup of user directories.

```
#!/bin/bash
SOURCE_DIR=/home/user
BACKUP_DIR=/backup/user_$(date +%Y%m%d%H%M)

mkdir -p $BACKUP_DIR
cp -r $SOURCE_DIR/* $BACKUP_DIR/
```

The #!/bin/bash line specifies that the script should be run in the Bash shell. SOURCE_DIR and BACKUP_DIR are variables storing the source and backup directory paths respectively. This script creates a directory with the current timestamp and copies all files from the source to the backup directory.

2. System Administration

System administrators leverage Bash scripting for managing user accounts, configuring system settings, and scheduling tasks. Examples include:

- Adding, deleting, or modifying user accounts.
- Configuring network settings.

- Installing and updating software packages.
- Setting up cron jobs to perform tasks at specified times.

A script for adding a user might look like this:

```
#!/bin/bash
USERNAME=newuser
PASSWORD=password

useradd -m -p "$(openssl passwd -1 $PASSWORD)" $USERNAME
usermod -aG sudo $USERNAME
echo "User $USERNAME created and added to sudo group."
```

Here, useradd creates a new user with a home directory, and openssl encrypts the password. usermod adds the user to the sudo group, conferring administrative privileges.

3. Data Processing

Bash scripts can parse and process data in various formats, including text files, CSV, and log files. They are often used for:

- Extracting specific information from log files.
- Converting data between different formats.
- Summarizing or filtering large datasets.

Consider a script that processes a CSV file to extract and summarize information:

```
#!/bin/bash
CSV_FILE=data.csv
awk -F, '{sum+=$2} END {print "Total:", sum}' $CSV_FILE
```

Using awk, this script sums the values in the second column of a CSV file. -F, specifies the comma as a field separator.

4. Task Scheduling

Bash scripts can be scheduled using tools like cron to perform tasks at regular intervals or specific times. Examples include:

- Running system updates weekly.
- Cleaning up temporary files daily.
- Generating reports and sending them via email every month.

A cron job entry for running a backup script daily at midnight might look like:

```
0 0 * * * /path/to/backup_script.sh
```

This line in the crontab file schedules the execution of backup_script.sh at 00:00 every day.

5. Rapid Prototyping

Developers use Bash scripts for prototyping and testing simple algorithms and system behaviors before implementing them in more complex languages. This approach allows for quick iterations and immediate feedback.

Here is a basic example to calculate the factorial of a number:

```
#!/bin/bash
factorial() {
    if [ $1 -le 1 ]; then
        echo 1
    else
        prev=$(factorial $(( $1 - 1 )))
        echo $(( $1 * prev ))
    fi
}

number=5
result=$(factorial $number)
echo "Factorial of $number is $result"
```

This script defines a recursive function factorial to compute the factorial of a given number, demonstrating the ease of prototyping with Bash.

6. Interfacing with Other Programs and Scripts

Bash scripts act as glue scripts, integrating various programs and scripts to perform complex workflows. Examples include:

- Combining output from different commands and programs to form a report.
- Managing workflows in data processing pipelines.
- Calling Python, Perl, or other scripts to handle specific tasks within a larger Bash script.

Here's how a Bash script might call a Python script and process its output:

```
#!/bin/bash
PYTHON_OUTPUT=$(python3 /path/to/script.py)
echo "Python script output: $PYTHON_OUTPUT"
```

The output from the Python script is captured in the PYTHON_OUTPUT variable and then printed.

These examples demonstrate the power and flexibility of Bash scripting in automating diverse tasks, making it an invaluable tool in both administrative and development environments.

1.9 Overview of Bash Scripting Language

Bash scripting provides a powerful way to automate tasks and manage system operations. This section delves into the core elements and constructs of the Bash scripting language, ensuring a robust understanding of its capabilities and syntax.

Bash (short for Bourne Again SHell) is a Unix shell and command language written as a free software replacement for the Bourne shell. It is widely available on various Unix and Unix-like systems as the default login shell.

Variables and Constants

In Bash, variables store data that can be used and manipulated throughout the script. Variables are declared and initialized without the use of the = sign, unlike in many other programming languages.

```
#!/bin/bash
# Variable declaration
my_variable="Hello, World!"
echo $my_variable
```

Variables can hold numbers, strings, or the results of commands. They can be used directly within strings by preceding them with the $ symbol.

Special Variables and Environment Variables

Bash scripts can also leverage special variables and environment variables. Some commonly used special variables include:

- $_: The last argument of the previous command.
- $?: The exit status of the last command.
- $$: The process ID of the current script.
- $!: The process ID of the last background command.

Environment variables are global system properties accessible from any script or command line operation.

```
#!/bin/bash
# Environment variables
echo $HOME
echo $PATH
```

Flow Control Structures

Flow control structures in Bash allow scripts to make decisions and execute commands conditionally. This includes if-else statements, looping constructs, and case statements.

If-else statements execute commands based on conditions:

```
#!/bin/bash
# If-else structure
if [ -d /home/user ]; then
    echo "User directory exists"
else
    echo "User directory does not exist"
fi
```

Loops are fundamental for iterating over lists or performing repetitive tasks. Bash supports several loop constructs, including for, while, and until loops.

```
#!/bin/bash
# For loop example
for i in {1..5}; do
    echo "Iteration $i"
done

# While loop example
count=1
while [ $count -le 5 ]; do
    echo "Iteration $count"
    ((count++))
done
```

Case statements provide a method for conditional execution based on pattern matching:

```
#!/bin/bash
# Case statement example
read -p "Enter a number between 1 and 3: " num
case $num in
    1)
        echo "You entered one"
        ;;
    2)
        echo "You entered two"
        ;;
    3)
        echo "You entered three"
        ;;
```

```
    *)
        echo "Invalid number"
        ;;
esac
```

Functions

Bash functions allow you to group commands and call them as a single unit. This is useful for code reuse and organization.

```
#!/bin/bash
# Function definition and usage
my_function() {
    echo "Function execution"
}

my_function
```

Functions can accept parameters and return values, aiding in building modular scripts.

```
#!/bin/bash
# Function with parameters
greet() {
    echo "Hello, $1"
}

greet "Alice"
```

Debugging and Error Handling

Effective debugging and error handling are crucial in Bash scripting. The set command is particularly useful:

- set -e: Exit immediately if a command exits with a non-zero status.
- set -x: Print each command before executing it.
- set -u: Treat unset variables as an error.

Trap commands enable handling signals and cleaning up before a script exits. The following example demonstrates basic error handling using trap:

```
#!/bin/bash
# Error handling with trap
trap "echo 'An error occurred! Cleaning up...'" ERR

# Example command that fails
ls /nonexistent_directory
```

Input and Output

Bash scripts can read input from the user and other sources. The read command captures user input:

```
#!/bin/bash
# Read user input
read -p "Enter your name: " name
echo "Hello, $name"
```

Files can be used as input or output through redirection:

```
#!/bin/bash
# Redirect output to a file
echo "This is a test" > output.txt
```

Here documents (heredocs) offer a method for writing multi-line input within a script:

```
#!/bin/bash
# Here document example
cat <<EOF
This is a multi-line
input text using
here document.
EOF
```

Overall, mastering the elements discussed in this section will provide a strong foundation for writing efficient and powerful Bash scripts, enabling robust automation and system management.

1.10 Resources for Learning and Further Reading

To deepen your understanding of Bash scripting and to evolve from a beginner to an expert, utilizing a variety of resources is crucial. These resources encompass official documentation, books, online tutorials, forums, and interactive platforms. Each resource serves a unique purpose and caters to different aspects of Bash scripting, providing a structured pathway for continual learning.

- **Official GNU Bash Reference Manual:** The *GNU Bash Reference Manual*[1] is an indispensable resource. It offers comprehensive documentation of all features in the Bash shell. The manual covers built-in functions, shell variables, and syntax with detailed

[1]Available at https://www.gnu.org/software/bash/manual/bash.html

descriptions. It is highly recommended for users seeking an authoritative and in-depth understanding of Bash.

- **Advanced Bash-Scripting Guide:** Written by Mendel Cooper, the *Advanced Bash-Scripting Guide*[2] is an extensive tutorial and reference book. It is structured to cater to users at varying levels of proficiency, from beginners to advanced. The guide includes practical examples and exercises, making it an excellent resource for hands-on learning.

- **Books:** Several books provide extensive coverage of Bash scripting concepts:

  - *Learning the bash Shell* by Cameron Newham and Bill Rosenblatt, published by O'Reilly Media, is a fundamental book for beginners.
  - *Pro Bash Programming: Scripting the GNU/Linux Shell* by Chris F.A. Johnson and Jayant Varma offers advanced tips and techniques.
  - *Bash Pocket Reference: Help for Power Users and Sys Admins* by Arnold Robbins is a concise guide focusing on practical usage.

- **Online Platforms and Tutorials:** Interactive online platforms and tutorials can greatly enhance your learning experience:

  - *Codecademy*[3] offers an interactive Command Line course which includes Bash scripting basics.
  - *Coursera*[4] and *edX*[5] feature courses on shell scripting fundamentals, delivered by universities and industry professionals.
  - *LinuxConfig.org*[6] provides step-by-step tutorials for beginners.
  - *The Bash Academy*[7] focuses on educating people about Bash usage, offering both beginner and advanced tutorials.

---

[2]Available at http://www.tldp.org/LDP/abs/html/
[3]Available at https://www.codecademy.com/learn/learn-the-command-line
[4]Available at https://www.coursera.org/learn/shell-scripting
[5]Available at https://www.edx.org/learn/shell-scripts
[6]Available at https://linuxconfig.org/bash-scripting-tutorial-for-beginners
[7]Available at http://www.bash.academy/

- **Online Forums and Communities:** Participating in forums and communities can help you solve problems, share knowledge, and stay updated with the latest developments:
  - *Stack Overflow*[8] is a popular platform where you can ask questions and interact with other Bash users.
  - *Unix & Linux Stack Exchange*[9] is a community-driven site focused on Unix and Linux shell scripting queries.
  - *Reddit* has several subreddits such as https://www.reddit.com/r/bash/ where you can share scripts, ask questions, and collaborate with other users.
  - *The LinuxQuestions.org Bash Forum*[10] provides a dedicated forum for scripting issues, offering assistance from experienced users.
- **YouTube Channels:** Visual learning through tutorials on YouTube can offer step-by-step guidance:
  - *TheNetNinja*[11] features a series on Bash scripting for beginners.
  - *TutoriaLinux*[12] offers in-depth tutorials focusing on different aspects of Linux command line and Bash scripting.
  - *ProgrammingKnowledge*[13] provides a comprehensive Bash scripting tutorial series.

Incorporating a mix of these resources into your study regimen will provide a robust understanding of Bash scripting, helping you leverage its full potential in your projects. Choose resources that align with your learning style and progress at a pace that ensures conceptual clarity and practical proficiency.

[8] Available at https://stackoverflow.com/questions/tagged/bash
[9] Available at https://unix.stackexchange.com/
[10] Available at https://www.linuxquestions.org/questions/programming-9/bash/
[11] Find at https://www.youtube.com/c/TheNetNinja
[12] Find at https://www.youtube.com/c/tutoriaLinux
[13] Find at https://www.youtube.com/user/ProgrammingKnowledge

Chapter 2

Setting Up Your Environment

This chapter is focused on preparing the ideal environment for Bash scripting. It guides readers through selecting an appropriate operating system, installing Linux and Bash, and accessing the terminal. The chapter covers configuring the shell environment, understanding shell profiles, and essential software installations. It also explores setting up text editors, customizing the terminal, managing software with package managers, and maintaining a secure environment.

2.1 Choosing the Right Operating System

Choosing the appropriate operating system is essential for optimizing your workflow in Bash scripting. Several factors determine the most suitable choice, such as compatibility, support for Bash, system performance, and available tools and packages. This section elaborates on the primary considerations and recommends optimal operating systems for various scenarios.

- **Compatibility with Bash**

The core component of this decision is ensuring that the operating system natively supports Bash. Bash, originally developed for GNU/Linux, is most commonly associated with Unix-like systems, including various Linux distributions, macOS, and BSD.

- **Linux Distributions**

Linux distributions (distros) offer a robust and flexible environment for Bash scripting. Popular distros like Ubuntu, Fedora, Debian, and CentOS come with Bash pre-installed and provide extensive package repositories for additional software. The long-term support (LTS) versions of these distributions ensure stability for production environments.

```
# Checking Bash version on Linux
bash --version
```

GNU bash, version 5.0.17(1)-release (x86_64-pc-linux-gnu)

- **macOS**

macOS, being Unix-based, includes Bash by default, though newer versions (starting with macOS Catalina) use zsh as the default shell. Transitioning to Bash is straightforward with a simple configuration change. macOS supports most GNU utilities, making it a viable option for Bash scripting.

```
# Changing the default shell to Bash on macOS
chsh -s /bin/bash
```

- **BSD Variants**

BSD variants, such as FreeBSD, NetBSD, and OpenBSD, also provide native support for Bash. These systems are known for their performance and security, making them suitable for scripting tasks that require robust handling.

- **Windows Subsystem for Linux (WSL)**

For users bound to Windows, the Windows Subsystem for Linux (WSL) provides a way to run a full Linux environment directly within Windows. This environment includes Bash and allows access to Linux-compatible tools without the need for a virtual machine or dual boot setup.

```
# Installing WSL and a Linux distribution on Windows 10
wsl --install
```

```
Installing WSL and Ubuntu. This may take a few minutes...
```

- **System Performance and Requirements**

Different operating systems require varying levels of system resources. Linux distributions such as Alpine Linux or Arch Linux are lightweight and minimalist, making them suitable for systems with limited hardware resources. Conversely, distros with extensive graphical interfaces like Ubuntu and Fedora may require more robust hardware.

- **Ease of Use and Community Support**

Select an operating system that aligns with your expertise level. Ubuntu and Fedora offer more user-friendly interfaces and comprehensive documentation, making them ideal for beginners. Advanced users might prefer Arch Linux or Gentoo for greater control and optimization capabilities.

Extensive community support and documentation can significantly ease troubleshooting and learning. Operating systems like Ubuntu, Debian, and Fedora boast extensive user forums, wikis, and other resources.

- **Available tools and Packages**

The availability of tools and software packages is a crucial consideration. Linux distributions feature robust package managers (`apt`, `yum`, `dnf`, `pacman`, etc.) that facilitate the installation and management of software. These repos often include precompiled binaries, ensuring easy setup and maintenance.

```
# Installing software with apt on a Debian-based distro
sudo apt-get update
sudo apt-get install -y build-essential
```

```
Setting up build-essential (12.4ubuntu1) ...
```

macOS users can leverage package managers such as Homebrew or MacPorts to install essential GNU tools and other software.

```
# Installing Homebrew and wget on macOS
/bin/bash -c "$(curl -fsSL https://raw.githubusercontent.com/Homebrew/install/
    HEAD/install.sh)"
brew install wget
```

BSD systems have their own package managers, such as pkg for FreeBSD, offering extensive software collections compatible with their platform.

- **Security Considerations**

Any operating system must maintain a secure environment to ensure reliable scripting operations. Choose systems that receive frequent security updates and have dedicated security advisories. Debian, RHEL (Red Hat Enterprise Linux), and CentOS are known for their security practices and long-term support plans.

```
# Updating the system and applying security patches
sudo apt-get update
sudo apt-get upgrade
```

```
Reading package lists... Done
Building dependency tree
Reading state information... Done
The following packages will be upgraded:
  openssl
...
```

Given these considerations, the ideal operating system will depend on your specific needs, system capabilities, and proficiency level. For general purposes, Ubuntu LTS provides a balanced choice between stability, support, and ease of use. Advanced users might opt for Debian or Arch Linux for greater customization and control. Those bound to macOS or Windows can still create a capable scripting environment using the aforementioned methods.

2.2 Installing Linux and Bash

To prepare an ideal environment for Bash scripting, it is essential to properly install both Linux and Bash. This section will guide you through the process, ensuring that you have a functional setup to begin scripting.

1. Downloading the Linux Distribution

Selecting a suitable Linux distribution is the first step. Popular distributions for Bash scripting include Ubuntu, Fedora, and CentOS. The distribution choice depends on your specific needs and familiarity with the Linux environment.

To download Ubuntu:

- Go to the official Ubuntu website (https://ubuntu.com/download).
- Select the version you want to install (LTS versions are recommended for stability).
- Click on the "Download" button to get the ISO file.

2. Creating a Bootable USB Drive

Once the ISO file is downloaded, create a bootable USB drive. Several tools can be used for this purpose, including Rufus (Windows) and dd (Linux). Example using dd:

```
sudo dd if=~/Downloads/ubuntu.iso of=/dev/sdX bs=4M
```

In this command, replace /Downloads/ubuntu.iso with the path to your downloaded ISO file and /dev/sdX with your USB drive's identifier.

3. Booting from the USB Drive

Insert the bootable USB drive into your system and restart it. Enter the BIOS/UEFI settings (usually by pressing Esc, F2, F10, or Del during startup) and configure the boot order to boot from the USB drive first. Save and exit the BIOS settings to proceed to the installation menu.

4. Installing Linux

Follow the on-screen instructions to install Linux. Key steps include:

- Select your language and keyboard layout.
- Choose Install Ubuntu or the equivalent option in other distributions.
- Configure your network settings.
- Choose installation type (opt for Erase disk and install Ubuntu or Install alongside if you have another OS).
- Create your user account and set up your computer's name and password.
- Wait for the installation to complete, then restart your system.

5. Post-Installation Setup

After rebooting, you might need to remove the USB drive and log in with the user account you created. Once logged in, it is crucial to update your system:

```
sudo apt update
sudo apt upgrade
```

6. Verifying Bash Installation

Most Linux distributions come with Bash pre-installed. Verify the installation by opening the terminal and checking the version:

```
bash --version
```

A typical output might look like:

```
GNU bash, version 5.0.17(1)-release (x86_64-pc-linux-gnu)
```

7. Installing Bash (if not pre-installed)

In cases where Bash is not installed, or you need a specific version:

- On Debian-based distributions (Ubuntu):

  ```
  sudo apt install bash
  ```

- On RPM-based distributions (Fedora/CentOS):

  ```
  sudo dnf install bash
  ```

8. Configuring Bash as the Default Shell

Verify and set Bash as the default shell using the chsh command:

```
chsh -s /bin/bash
```

Log out and log back in for changes to take effect. Verify the current shell:

```
echo $SHELL
```

It should output:

```
/bin/bash
```

Following these steps ensures a robust Linux environment with Bash ready for scripting. Proper installation and configuration are foundational to achieving proficiency in Bash scripting.

2.3 Accessing the Terminal

The terminal, also known as the command line, is a critical interface for executing Bash scripts and performing numerous administrative tasks. Understanding how to access and utilize the terminal is fundamental for effective Bash scripting.

Accessing the Terminal on Different Operating Systems

For various operating systems, the procedure to access the terminal varies. Below are the steps for accessing the terminal on some of the most commonly used operating systems.

Linux: Most Linux distributions have a terminal application readily available. You can launch the terminal by searching for Terminal in your application menu. Alternatively, you can open the terminal using key combinations such as Ctrl + Alt + T.

macOS: On macOS, the terminal is also easily accessible. Open the Finder, navigate to the Applications directory, and then to the Utilities folder. Here you will find the Terminal application. You can also use Spotlight by pressing Cmd + Space and typing "Terminal" to quickly launch it.

Windows: Windows users can access a terminal-like interface through PowerShell or the Command Prompt. However, for a more Unix-like experience, it is recommended to use Windows Subsystem for Linux (WSL). After installing WSL, you can open a Linux terminal from the start menu.

Basic Terminal Commands

Once you have accessed the terminal, it's essential to familiarize yourself with some basic commands to navigate and manipulate files and directories.

```
# Display the current working directory
pwd

# List files and directories in the current directory
ls

# Change to another directory
cd /path/to/directory

# Create a new directory
mkdir new_directory

# Remove a file
rm filename
```

```
# Remove a directory and its contents
rm -r directory_name

# Copy files or directories
cp source destination

# Move files or directories
mv source destination

# Display the contents of a file
cat filename

# Clear the terminal screen
clear
```

The pwd (print working directory) command is used to display the current directory you are working in. The ls command lists the contents of the current directory. The cd command changes your current directory. For example, cd /home/user/Documents would navigate to the Documents directory within the /home/user directory.

Creating a new directory can be achieved with the mkdir command. Removing files and directories is done using rm, and if you want to remove a directory and its contents, you would use rm -r. Copying and moving files are performed with the cp and mv commands, respectively.

To display the contents of a file, you can use the cat command. Finally, the clear command is useful when you want to clear the terminal screen.

Using Terminal for Bash Scripting

The terminal enables the execution of Bash scripts and various command-line utilities. To run a Bash script, navigate to the directory containing your script and use the following command:

```
# Navigate to the script's directory
cd /path/to/script

# Make the script executable
chmod +x script_name.sh

# Execute the script
./script_name.sh
```

First, navigate to the directory where your script is located using the cd command. The chmod +x command makes the script executable. Finally, run the script with ./script_name.sh.

Terminal Shortcuts and Efficiencies

Several shortcuts and tips can make using the terminal more efficient.

- Use Tab for autocompletion of commands and file names.

- Use Ctrl + C to terminate a running command.
- Use Ctrl + R to search through your command history.
- Use the Up and Down arrow keys to cycle through previously used commands.
- Use && to execute multiple commands sequentially. For example:

```
command1 && command2
```

- Use | (pipe) to pass the output of one command as input to another command. For example:

```
ls | grep pattern
```

Navigating the terminal efficiently not only saves time but also enhances your ability to manage and script effectively. Practice consistently and explore more complex commands as you become comfortable with the basics.

2.4 Configuring Your Shell Environment

Configuring your shell environment is a crucial step in mastering Bash scripting. A well-configured shell can significantly enhance your productivity and scripting efficiency. This section will guide you through the essential aspects of setting up your shell environment.

The shell environment consists of various configurations and settings that dictate how your shell behaves. These configurations are generally managed through environment variables and shell options. We'll cover setting environment variables, customizing the prompt, enabling useful shell options, and making your configurations persistent.

1. Setting Environment Variables

Environment variables are key-value pairs that can affect the way running processes will behave on your system. Common environment variables include PATH, HOME, and USER.

To set an environment variable, use the export command:

```
export VARIABLE_NAME=value
```

For example, setting the PATH variable to include a new directory:

```
export PATH=\$PATH:/new/directory/path
```

The above command appends /new/directory/path to the existing PATH. Verifying the new PATH value can be done by echoing the variable:

```
echo \$PATH
```

The output will show the updated PATH:

```
/usr/local/bin:/usr/bin:/bin:/new/directory/path
```

2. Customizing the Prompt

A customized prompt can provide useful information at a glance. The prompt is controlled by the PS1 environment variable. To set a simple prompt showing the current user, hostname, and working directory, use:

```
export PS1='\u@\h:\w\$ '
```

In this string, \u represents the username, \h the hostname, and \w the current working directory. The dollar sign ($) signifies the prompt.

After setting the PS1 variable, the prompt will look like this:

```
user@hostname:/current/directory$
```

For more advanced customizations, you can include colors and special characters. For instance:

```
export PS1='\[\e[0;32m\]\u@\h:\w\$ \[\e[0m\]'
```

This setting will display the prompt text in green, where \e[0;32m begins the green color and \e[0m resets the color back to default.

3. Enabling Useful Shell Options

Bash offers several options that can enhance the user experience and make scripting easier. Some useful options include:

- set -o noclobber: Prevents overwriting files with the > redirection operator.
- set -o ignoreeof: Prevents the shell from exiting when Ctrl-D (End-of-File) is pressed.

- set -o vi or set -o emacs: Enables vi-style or emacs-style command line editing.

To enable these options, use the set command:

```
set -o noclobber
set -o ignoreeof
set -o vi
```

These settings change the behavior of the shell, making it safer and more convenient to use.

4. Making Your Configurations Persistent

To ensure that your environment variables, prompt settings, and shell options persist across sessions, add them to your shell's configuration files. For bash, these files are typically ~/.bashrc or ~/.bash_profile.

Open your ~/.bashrc file in a text editor and add your configuration settings:

```
# Environment variables
export PATH=\$PATH:/new/directory/path

# Custom prompt
export PS1='\u@\h:\w\$ '

# Shell options
set -o noclobber
set -o ignoreeof
set -o vi
```

Save the file and reload it with:

```
source ~/.bashrc
```

By structuring your shell environment this way, you ensure that your configurations are consistently applied every time you start a new shell session.

A properly configured shell environment establishes a solid foundation for efficient and effective Bash scripting.

2.5 Understanding Shell Profiles and Configuration Files

Shell profiles and configuration files are instrumental in customizing and optimizing your scripting environment. These files allow users to define environment variables, set aliases, configure path settings, and modulate other shell behaviors, ensuring that the environment is suited to the user's needs upon startup. Bash uses various initialization files, and understanding their hierarchy and functionality aids in effective environment management.

.bashrc is one of the most commonly used configuration files for Bash. It is executed for non-login interactive shells. When a new terminal window or tab is opened, .bashrc is sourced. This file is typically situated in the user's home directory and can be used to set up custom environment settings, aliases, and functions.

```
# Sample .bashrc configuration file
# ~/.bashrc

# Source global definitions
if [ -f /etc/bashrc ]; then
    . /etc/bashrc
fi

# User specific environment and startup programs
PATH=$PATH:$HOME/bin
export PATH

# Aliases and functions
alias ll='ls -la'
alias gs='git status'
```

The /etc/bashrc file is sourced globally for all users, ensuring system-wide configurations are applied first. Users can then override or append settings in their personal .bashrc. The $PATH variable is extended to include the user's $HOME/bin directory, ensuring any executables stored there are easily accessible. Aliases like ll for a detailed list view and gs for git status can significantly streamline common tasks.

The .bash_profile is another crucial file. This file is executed for login shells. Linux typically distinguishes login and non-login shells, each serving different initialization routines. Prioritization of reading the profile files is:

- The /etc/profile is read first
- followed by the .bash_profile in the user's home directory
- If .bash_profile is not found, Bash attempts to read .bash_login
- and subsequently .profile, if they exist.

```
# ~/.bash_profile
```

```
# Get the aliases and functions
if [ -f ~/.bashrc ]; then
    . ~/.bashrc
fi

# Add personal scripts to PATH
PATH=$PATH:$HOME/scripts
export PATH

# Set up Ruby environment
export GEM_HOME="$HOME/.gems"
export PATH="$HOME/.gems/bin:$PATH"
```

The example above demonstrates sourcing .bashrc within .bash_profile to maintain consistency between login and interactive shells. This approach avoids duplicative configuration, ensuring all shell types have consistent environment settings. By adding the user's $HOME/scripts directory to the $PATH, executables located in $HOME/scripts become accessible. Furthermore, Ruby gem paths can be configured in .bash_profile, aligning Ruby environments with the user account.

Another essential file is .profile, commonly utilized by many Unix-like systems for compatibility between different shell types and environments. Unlike .bash_profile, it is more shell-agnostic and can work with different shells like sh, dash, or ksh.

```
# ~/.profile

# Setting PATH for general shell usage
if [ -d "$HOME/bin" ] ; then
    PATH="$HOME/bin:$PATH"
fi

# Custom environment variables
export EDITOR=nano
export HISTIGNORE="&:ls:[bf]g:exit"
```

In this instance, .profile checks if the $HOME/bin directory exists and, if so, adds it to $PATH. This ensures that any binaries placed in the bin directory are executable from any shell. The EDITOR environment variable is set to nano, making nano the default text editor for command-line utilities that rely on the $EDITOR variable. Additionally, HISTIGNORE is configured to exclude commands such as ls and exit from being stored in the command history, enhancing privacy and usability.

When configuring a Bash environment, understanding the sequence of execution for these profile files is critical. The hierarchy for login shells typically starts with /etc/profile, then proceeds to .bash_profile, .bash_login, and .profile, in that order. For non-login, interactive shells, .bashrc is primarily used, and it is standard practice to source .bashrc within .bash_profile for consistent behavior across shell sessions.

Moreover, users can leverage .bash_logout to execute commands upon logging out from a shell session. This file often contains commands for cleanup activities or custom logout procedures.

```
# ~/.bash_logout

# Clear the terminal screen to improve privacy
clear
```

In this example, the clear command is included to clear the terminal screen upon logout, safeguarding any potentially sensitive command history from view.

By mastering these configuration files, users can tailor their shell environments precisely to their needs, automate routine tasks, and optimize their scripting environment, thus enhancing their overall efficiency and productivity.

2.6 Installing Essential Software and Tools

Installing the necessary software and tools is a crucial step in setting up an environment conducive to effective Bash scripting. This section provides detailed instructions on acquiring and configuring essential utilities that will enhance your scripting capabilities.

The foundational toolset for Bash scripting includes package managers, text editors, version control systems, debugging tools, and specific utilities that facilitate script development. Before proceeding with installation, ensure your system is up-to-date to avoid compatibility issues. For systems using apt, such as Debian or Ubuntu, run the following commands:

```
sudo apt update && sudo apt upgrade
```

For systems using yum, such as CentOS or RHEL:

```
sudo yum check-update && sudo yum update
```

Package Managers

While most systems come with a default package manager, familiarity with it is essential. Not only does the package manager handle software installation, but it also manages dependencies, updates software, and maintains a record of installed packages. The following are the most common package managers:

- apt for Debian-based distributions.
- yum for RHEL-based distributions.
- dnf, a modern replacement for yum.
- zypper for SUSE-based distributions.
- pacman for Arch-based distributions.

If your system runs apt, use:

```
sudo apt install -y build-essential
```

If your system uses yum, use:

```
sudo yum groupinstall "Development Tools"
```

Text Editors

Choosing the right text editor can improve productivity. Some popular options include:

- vim
- nano
- gedit
- emacs
- VS Code

Install vim through your package manager:

```
sudo apt install vim
```

To install nano:

```
sudo apt install nano
```

For gedit:

```
sudo apt install gedit
```

VS Code can be installed by first downloading the package and then using the package manager:

```
wget -qO- https://packages.microsoft.com/keys/microsoft.asc | gpg --dearmor >
    microsoft.gpg
sudo install -o root -g root -m 644 microsoft.gpg /etc/apt/trusted.gpg.d/
sudo sh -c 'echo "deb [arch=amd64] https://packages.microsoft.com/repos/vscode
    stable main" > /etc/apt/sources.list.d/vscode.list'
sudo apt update
sudo apt install code
```

Version Control Systems

Git is the standard version control system that is essential for managing scripts and collaborative projects:

```
sudo apt install git
```

To confirm the installation, check the Git version:

```
git --version
```

Debugging Tools

Debugging is a vital part of scripting, and bash provides built-in debugging options. For more advanced debugging, install tools such as:

- gdb
- strace

To install gdb:

```
sudo apt install gdb
```

To install strace:

```
sudo apt install strace
```

Additional Utilities

Other utilities that might enhance scripting include:

- curl for transferring data with URLs:

  ```
  sudo apt install curl
  ```

- wget for downloading files from the web:

  ```
  sudo apt install wget
  ```

- jq for processing JSON data:

```
sudo apt install jq
```

- htop for monitoring system resources:

```
sudo apt install htop
```

Verifying the installations confirms the availability and correct setup of these tools. Use the –version or -V option with each installed tool to check its version:

```
vim --version
nano --version
gedit --version
code --version
git --version
gdb --version
strace --version
curl --version
wget --version
jq --version
htop --version
```

By ensuring all essential software and tools are correctly installed, your environment will be well-prepared to handle advanced Bash scripting tasks effectively.

2.7 Setting Up a Text Editor for Scripting

When preparing your environment for Bash scripting, selecting and configuring a text editor that matches your workflow and preferences is essential. A suitable text editor can significantly enhance productivity by providing features such as syntax highlighting, auto-completion, and integrated terminal support.

There are several popular text editors, each with unique features suitable for Bash scripting. Two of the most widely used editors are Vim and Visual Studio Code (VS Code). This section provides a detailed overview of installing, configuring, and utilizing these editors for effective scripting.

Installing Vim

Vim is a highly configurable text editor built to enable efficient text editing. It is an improved version of the vi editor, with added functionalities. Vim is available on most Unix-like operating systems. To install Vim:

```
# On Debian-based systems like Ubuntu
sudo apt-get update
```

```
sudo apt-get install vim

# On RHEL-based systems like Fedora
sudo dnf install vim
```

Once installed, Vim can be started from the terminal by simply typing:

```
vim
```

.vimrc Configuration: Vim's behavior can be customized by editing the ~/.vimrc file. Below is a typical configuration that enhances Vim's usability for Bash scripting:

```
set nu " Show line numbers
syntax on " Enable syntax highlighting
set tabstop=4 " Number of spaces for a tab
set shiftwidth=4 " Number of spaces to use for autoindent
set expandtab " Convert tabs to spaces
set ai " Enable auto-indenting
set bg=dark " Use a dark background
```

To enable this configuration, create or edit the ~/.vimrc file by:

```
vim ~/.vimrc
```

and then paste the above configuration into the file and save it.

Installing Visual Studio Code

Visual Studio Code (VS Code) is a powerful, open-source code editor developed by Microsoft. It offers extensive support for various languages and platforms, including Bash scripting. To install VS Code:

```
# On Debian-based systems like Ubuntu
sudo apt update
sudo apt install wget gpg
wget -qO- https://packages.microsoft.com/keys/microsoft.asc | gpg --dearmor >
    packages.microsoft.gpg
sudo install -o root -g root -m 644 packages.microsoft.gpg /usr/share/keyrings/
sudo sh -c 'echo "deb [arch=$(dpkg --print-architecture) signed-by=/usr/share/keyrings
    /packages.microsoft.gpg] https://packages.microsoft.com/repos/vscode stable
    main" > /etc/apt/sources.list.d/vscode.list'
sudo apt install apt-transport-https
sudo apt update
sudo apt install code

# On RHEL-based systems like Fedora
sudo rpm --import https://packages.microsoft.com/keys/microsoft.asc
sudo sh -c 'echo -e "[code]\nname=Visual Studio Code\nbaseurl=https://packages.
    microsoft.com/yumrepos/vscode\nenabled=1\ntype=rpm-md\ngpgcheck=1\
    ngpgkey=https://packages.microsoft.com/keys/microsoft.asc" > /etc/yum.repos.d
    /vscode.repo'
dnf check-update
sudo dnf install code
```

Once installed, VS Code can be opened from the terminal by typing:

```
code
```

Settings and Extensions VS Code can be customized by installing extensions and configuring settings. To enhance the experience of Bash scripting, consider adding:

- Bash IDE extension for code completion and debugging.
- Bash Beautify extension for formatting scripts.
- ShellCheck for static analysis and linting.

To install an extension, press Ctrl+P to open the command palette, type ext install <extension-name>, and press Enter.

VS Code settings can be configured by navigating to File > Preferences > Settings and searching for the preferred settings. For example, to set tab size to 4 spaces for Bash files, add the following entry to the settings:

```
"[shellscript]": {
    "editor.tabSize": 4,
    "editor.insertSpaces": true
}
```

Integrating Terminals: VS Code supports integrated terminals, which can be accessed via View > Terminal or by pressing Ctrl+`. This feature enables running and debugging scripts directly within the editor.

Using Other Editors There are other text editors popular among Bash script developers, such as GNU Emacs, Sublime Text, and Atom. Each editor has its installation procedures and unique features. Regardless of the editor chosen, it is crucial to configure it in a manner that best suits your development style and enhances your scripting efficiency.

Vim and VS Code are commonly preferred for their robust configurability and extensive feature sets, making them excellent choices for proficient Bash scripting.

2.8 Customizing Your Terminal

Customizing your terminal environment is an essential step in optimizing your workflow and making your scripting activities more efficient and enjoyable. This section introduces several key aspects of terminal customization, including customizing the terminal prompt, setting environment variables, and enhancing the terminal's appearance and functionality using various tools.

Customizing the Terminal Prompt

The terminal prompt is the string of characters displayed when the shell is ready to accept a command. By default, the prompt might only display the username and hostname. However, customizing the prompt can provide valuable context, such as the current working directory or the current Git branch. For instance, the default prompt might look like this:

```
user@hostname:~$
```

To customize the terminal prompt, you can modify the PS1 variable in your shell configuration file (e.g., .bashrc for Bash). Here is an example that includes the username, hostname, and current working directory:

```
export PS1="\u@\h:\w$ "
```

In this script:

- \u represents the username.
- \h represents the hostname.
- \w represents the current working directory.

The effect of this customization can be verified by opening a new terminal session or sourcing the .bashrc file:

```
source ~/.bashrc
```

Setting Environment Variables

Environment variables play a crucial role in defining the behavior of the shell and its applications. Common environment variables include PATH, HOME, and EDITOR. The PATH variable, for example, lists directories to be searched for executable files. You can customize the PATH variable in your shell configuration file:

```
export PATH=$PATH:/your/custom/path
```

This appends /your/custom/path to the existing PATH variable. Ensure you use the correct syntax to avoid overwriting the current PATH.

Another useful environment variable is EDITOR, which specifies the default text editor for operations such as editing crontab files:

```
export EDITOR=nano
```

Enhancing Terminal Appearance and Functionality

There are numerous tools and tweaks available to enhance the terminal's appearance and functionality, including color schemes, plugins, and utilities.

Color Schemes and Themes

Using color can significantly improve readability and productivity. For instance, directory listings can be color-coded to distinguish files from directories quickly. The LS_COLORS variable controls the colorization of the output from the ls command. You can set this variable by adding a line to your shell configuration file or by using a tool like dircolors:

```
eval $(dircolors -b)
```

Installing and Using Powerline

Powerline is a popular status line plugin that provides a rich, sophisticated look to the terminal prompt. It includes segment-based enhancements such as Git branch information and system load metrics. To install Powerline, use the package manager:

```
sudo apt-get install powerline
```

Add the following lines to your shell configuration file to enable Powerline:

```
if [ -f `pip show powerline-status | grep Location | cut -d " " -f 2`/powerline/bindings/
    bash/powerline.sh ]; then
  . `pip show powerline-status | grep Location | cut -d " " -f 2`/powerline/bindings/
      bash/powerline.sh
fi
```

Customizing with Zsh and Oh-My-Zsh

For those seeking even more customization options, switching to the Zsh shell along with the Oh-My-Zsh framework can be highly beneficial. Zsh provides advanced features like improved tab completion, better history management, and plugin support.

To install Zsh:

```
sudo apt-get install zsh
```

To set Zsh as the default shell:

```
chsh -s $(which zsh)
```

After ensuring Zsh is installed, install Oh-My-Zsh:

```
sh -c "$(curl -fsSL https://raw.githubusercontent.com/ohmyzsh/ohmyzsh/master/tools/
    install.sh)"
```

Oh-My-Zsh includes numerous themes and plugins. For example, to change the theme, edit the ZSH_THEME variable in the .zshrc file:

```
ZSH_THEME="agnoster"
```

Plugins can be enabled by listing them in the plugins section of the .zshrc file:

```
plugins=(git zsh-syntax-highlighting zsh-autosuggestions)
```

These enhancements are immediately reflected upon restarting the terminal or re-sourcing the configuration file:

```
source ~/.zshrc
```

Employing Aliases and Functions

Aliases and functions can simplify and speed up command-line tasks. For example, an alias can create a shortcut for a frequently used command:

```
alias ll="ls -la"
```

Functions provide more advanced scripting capabilities within the shell:

```
extract() {
    if [ -f $1 ] ; then
        case $1 in
            *.tar.bz2) tar xjf $1 ;;
            *.tar.gz) tar xzf $1 ;;
            *.bz2) bunzip2 $1 ;;
            *.rar) unrar e $1 ;;
            *.gz) gunzip $1 ;;
            *.tar) tar xf $1 ;;
            *.tbz2) tar xjf $1 ;;
            *.tgz) tar xzf $1 ;;
            *.zip) unzip $1 ;;
            *.Z) uncompress $1 ;;
            *) echo "don't know how to extract '$1'..." ;;
        esac
    else
        echo "'$1' is not a valid file!"
    fi
}
```

By customizing the terminal environment, users can achieve a more pleasant and efficient workspace tailored to their specific needs and preferences, enabling them to perform tasks more effectively.

2.9 Managing Software with Package Managers

Efficient software management is paramount for a seamless scripting environment. Package managers significantly simplify the installation, updating, and removal of software. In this section, we will explore the different types of package managers available, their functionalities, and how to leverage them for optimal system configuration.

Package managers are categorized into two primary types: binary package managers and source-based package managers. Binary package managers manage precompiled software binaries, facilitating rapid installation without the need for further compilation. Examples include apt, dnf, and yum. In contrast, source-based package managers, such as portage in Gentoo, download source code and compile it locally, offering more customization at the cost of longer installation times.

APT (Advanced Package Tool)

APT is the package manager utilized by Debian-based distributions such as Ubuntu. Below is a common set of commands essential for managing software using apt:

```
sudo apt update
sudo apt install <package_name>
sudo apt remove <package_name>
sudo apt upgrade
sudo apt autoremove
```

- apt update: Refreshes the list of available packages and their versions, ensuring that the package information is up to date.
- apt install <package_name>: Installs the specified package.
- apt remove <package_name>: Uninstalls the specified package without deleting configuration files.
- apt upgrade: Upgrades all the installed packages to their latest versions.

- apt autoremove: Removes packages installed as dependencies that are no longer required.

DNF (Dandified Yum)

DNF is the next-generation package manager for RPM-based distributions like Fedora and Red Hat Enterprise Linux (RHEL). Key commands to manage software using dnf include:

```
sudo dnf check-update
sudo dnf install <package_name>
sudo dnf remove <package_name>
sudo dnf upgrade
sudo dnf clean all
```

- dnf check-update: Checks for any available updates for installed packages.
- dnf install <package_name>: Installs the specified package.
- dnf remove <package_name>: Removes the specified package.
- dnf upgrade: Upgrades all installed packages to the latest versions.
- dnf clean all: Clears the repository cache and any remaining metadata.

YUM (Yellowdog Updater, Modified)

YUM, although largely replaced by dnf, is still prevalent in older RPM-based systems. It performs similar functions:

```
sudo yum check-update
sudo yum install <package_name>
sudo yum remove <package_name>
sudo yum update
sudo yum clean all
```

For both binary and source-based package managers, understanding dependency management is crucial. Dependencies are additional packages required by the primary package for proper functionality. Failure to resolve dependencies may lead to broken installations.

Dependency Management

Most modern package managers automatically resolve dependencies. However, issues can still arise. Below is an example scenario using apt, illustrating how to manage dependencies manually if automatic resolution fails:

```
sudo apt install <package_name> --fix-broken
```

Using the –fix-broken option helps resolve any dependency issues that might have occurred during installation.

Repositories

Package managers rely on repositories, which are collections of software packages. Managing repositories is essential for accessing the latest versions and additional software not included by default. For apt, managing repositories involves editing the sources.list file:

```
sudo nano /etc/apt/sources.list
```

Add or remove repository URLs based on your requirements. After editing, update the repository list:

```
sudo apt update
```

Similarly, repositories for dnf are managed in the /etc/yum.repos.d/ directory, where each repository configuration is stored as a .repo file.

Algorithm 1: Enabling a Repository in DNF

Data: Repository configuration file
Result: Repository enabled in DNF

Open the repository file for editing;
sudo nano /etc/yum.repos.d/<repo_name>.repo;
Set enabled=1 to enable the repository;
[repository_id];
name=Some Repository;
baseurl=http://url.to/repository;
enabled=1;
gpgcheck=1;
gpgkey=http://url.to/repo_gpg_key;
Save and close the file;
Update the repository list;
sudo dnf check-update;

Security Considerations

While managing software, it is essential to ensure that the sources and repositories used are trustworthy. Using measures like gpgcheck and verifying package signatures can prevent the installation of malicious software. Regularly updating the package manager and installed packages mitigates vulnerabilities that could be exploited.

Overall, mastering the use of package managers is a fundamental skill for maintaining an efficient, secure, and up-to-date scripting environment. Proficiency in this aspect will significantly enhance the stability and performance of your system.

2.10 Keeping Your Environment Secure

Security is paramount in any computing environment, and your scripting environment is no exception. Ensuring that your Bash environment is secure involves several layers, including user permissions, secure authentication methods, environment variable management, and setting proper file permissions. This section will delve into these aspects, providing a comprehensive guide to securing your Bash scripting environment.

User Permissions

Begin by limiting user permissions. The principle of least privilege dictates that users should have only the permissions necessary to perform their tasks. To implement this, use the chmod, chown, and chgrp commands to control access to files and directories.

In Bash, file permissions are often modified using the chmod command. For instance:

```
$ chmod 700 script.sh
```

The above command sets the permissions so that only the user can read, write, and execute the file script.sh.

User ownership and group ownership of files can be changed with chown and chgrp respectively. For instance:

```
$ sudo chown user:user script.sh
$ sudo chgrp usergroup script.sh
```

These commands can restrict the access further based on ownership, enhancing security.

Secure Authentication

SSH (Secure Shell) is commonly used for secure remote logins. Key-based authentication is more secure than password authentication. Generate SSH keys using the ssh-keygen utility and configure them as follows:

```
$ ssh-keygen -t rsa -b 4096 -C "your_email@example.com"
$ ssh-copy-id user@remote_host
```

Disable root login via SSH and password authentication by editing the /etc/ssh/sshd_config file:

```
$ sudo nano /etc/ssh/sshd_config
```

Set the following parameters:

```
PermitRootLogin no
PasswordAuthentication no
```

Restart the SSH service to apply changes:

```
$ sudo systemctl restart ssh
```

Environment Variable Management

Environment variables are used extensively in Bash scripts. Sensitive information such as passwords or tokens should never be hard-coded. Utilize environment variables securely by restricting their scope and access. Use export to limit variable visibility:

```
$ export SECRET_API_KEY="your_secret_key"
```

For sensitive data, consider using environment variable files that source sensitive values securely:

```
#!/bin/bash
set -a
source /path/to/env_file
set +a
```

Ensure the environment variable file is secure by restricting its permissions:

```
$ chmod 600 /path/to/env_file
```

File Permissions

File permission management is critical to protecting scripts and their execution environment. Use the umask command to set default permissions for newly created files and directories. For example, to set a more restrictive umask of 027:

```
$ umask 027
```

The above setting ensures that new files are created with permissions of 750, disallowing others from reading the files.

Using sudo Securely

Executables that require elevated privileges should be managed with sudo rather than switching to the root user. Configure sudo to grant the minimum required permissions by editing the /etc/sudoers file using visudo:

```
$ sudo visudo
```

Add or modify entries to limit the commands that users can run. For instance:

```
user ALL=(ALL) NOPASSWD: /usr/bin/somecommand
```

This ensures that the user can run somecommand without needing the root password.

Disabling Unused Services

Reduce the attack surface by disabling unused services and unnecessary network protocols. Use systemctl to disable and stop non-essential services. For example, to disable the FTP service:

```
$ sudo systemctl stop vsftpd
$ sudo systemctl disable vsftpd
```

Regular Software Updates

Ensure your system and software, including Bash, are up to date with security patches. Use your package manager to regularly update your system. For Debian-based systems:

```
$ sudo apt update && sudo apt upgrade
```

For Red Hat-based systems:

```
$ sudo yum update
```

Monitoring and Logging

Regular monitoring and logging are vital for detecting unauthorized access or anomalies. Configure rsyslog or syslog-ng to log system activities and review these logs periodically. Enhance monitoring with tools such as fail2ban to protect against brute-force attacks.

Enable and configure fail2ban:

```
$ sudo apt install fail2ban
```

```
$ sudo nano /etc/fail2ban/jail.local
```

Add configurations to protect SSH:

```
[sshd]
enabled = true
port = ssh
filter = sshd
logpath = /var/log/auth.log
maxretry = 6
```

Restart fail2ban for changes to take effect:

```
$ sudo systemctl restart fail2ban
```

Securing your environment is a continuous process that incorporates best practices and proactive measures. By comprehensively controlling user permissions, employing strong authentication methods, managing environment variables securely, enforcing strict file permissions, using sudo judiciously, disabling unnecessary services, keeping your system updated, and implementing robust monitoring and logging protocols, you can effectively protect your Bash scripting environment from potential security threats.

Chapter 3

Basic Bash Syntax and Commands

This chapter delves into the fundamental syntax and essential commands of Bash scripting. It covers running basic commands, using command options and arguments, and working with command aliases. Readers will learn to navigate the filesystem, understand file permissions, and utilize wildcards and globbing. The chapter also addresses input and output redirection, piping and chaining commands, and command substitution, providing a solid foundation in Bash scripting.

3.1 Understanding the Basic Syntax

In Bash scripting, the structure and syntax are foundational elements that enable effective script development. Bash scripts are essentially sequences of commands executed by the Bash shell. This section covers the crucial aspects of basic syntax in Bash scripting to ensure clarity and consistency in script writing.

A Bash script typically starts with a shebang ($\#!/\mathrm{bin}/\mathrm{bash}$) at the top of the file, indicating that the script should be executed with the Bash interpreter. It is crucial to include the shebang in every Bash script to avoid execution errors, especially in environments with multiple scripting languages.

```
#!/bin/bash
# This is a comment
echo "Hello, World!"
```

In the example above, the first line, #!/bin/bash, specifies that the script should be run using the Bash shell. Comments are preceded by the # character and are ignored by the interpreter, helping to annotate and document the script. The echo command prints the string "Hello, World!" to the terminal.

Variable declaration and usage form the backbone of dynamic script execution. Variables store data values and are declared without any explicit data type. The assignment operator (=) is used to set the variable's value, and variables are referenced by prefixing a dollar sign ($).

```
#!/bin/bash
# Variable declaration and usage
greeting="Hello"
name="Alice"
echo "$greeting, $name!"
```

The example above declares two variables, greeting and name, and uses them within the echo statement. Note the usage of double quotes to ensure that variable values are correctly expanded during execution.

Bash scripts often include control structures such as conditions and loops, allowing for decision-making and repetitive tasks. Conditional statements typically use if, then, else, and fi keywords, encapsulating the logic to be executed based on specific criteria.

```
#!/bin/bash
# Conditional statement
num=10
if [ $num -eq 10 ]; then
    echo "The number is 10."
else
    echo "The number is not 10."
fi
```

In this example, if checks whether the variable num equals 10 using the -eq operator. If true, the script prints "The number is 10." Otherwise, it prints "The number is not 10." Note the use of square brackets [] to denote the condition being evaluated.

Looping constructs in Bash include for, while, and until loops, each providing different mechanisms to iterate over a set of values or continue execution while certain conditions hold true.

```
#!/bin/bash
# For loop example
for i in 1 2 3 4 5; do
```

```
    echo "Iteration $i"
done

# While loop example
counter=1
while [ $counter -le 5 ]; do
    echo "Counter: $counter"
    ((counter++))
done
```

In the for loop example, the loop iterates over a list of values (1 to 5) and prints each iteration value. The while loop continues to execute as long as the condition [$counter -le 5] holds true, incrementing the counter variable in every iteration using the ((counter++)) syntax.

Functions in Bash scripts modularize code into reusable blocks, improving readability and maintainability. A function is declared using the function keyword followed by the function name and curly braces enclosing the function body.

```
#!/bin/bash
# Function example
function greet() {
    local name=$1
    echo "Hello, $name!"
}

greet "Bob"
```

The greet function takes an argument name and prints a greeting message. The local keyword ensures that the variable name is locally scoped within the function, preventing potential variable name conflicts. The function is then invoked with the argument "Bob".

Special characters and quoting mechanisms in Bash influence how the shell interprets the data. Double quotes (") allow variable expansion, single quotes (') preserve literal values without expansion, and backslashes (\) escape special characters.

To summarize, understanding the basic syntax of Bash scripting involves a thorough comprehension of the script structure, variable declarations, control structures, looping constructs, functions, and special characters handling. This foundational knowledge is imperative for writing efficient and effective Bash scripts.

3.2 Running Basic Commands

Running basic commands in Bash entails executing instructions that the shell interprets to perform specific tasks. These commands are foundational building blocks for more complex scripts and interactions with the system. Familiarity with basic commands is crucial for efficient navigation and manipulation of the filesystem, process management, and general system operations.

To execute a command in Bash, one typically types the command followed by the Enter key. The basic syntax for running a command is simply:

```
command [options] [arguments]
```

command represents the executable program or shell built-in, options modify the behavior of the command, and arguments specify the target upon which the command acts. Options often start with a hyphen (-), and arguments follow the options.

Examples:

1. A simple command without options or arguments:

```
echo "Hello, World!"
```

This command outputs the string "Hello, World!" to the terminal.

```
Hello, World!
```

2. A command with options and an argument:

```
ls -l /home/user/documents
```

Here, ls lists the contents of the directory specified by the argument /home/user/documents; the option -l provides a detailed listing.

```
total 0
-rw-r--r-- 1 user user 0 Mar 21 12:34 file1.txt
-rw-r--r-- 1 user user 0 Mar 21 12:34 file2.txt
```

Common Basic Commands:

1. pwd - Print Working Directory

```
pwd
```

Displays the current directory you are working in.

/home/user

2. cd - Change Directory

```
cd /home/user/documents
```

Changes the current directory to /home/user/documents.

3. ls - List Directory Contents

```
ls
```

Lists files and directories in the current directory.

file1.txt file2.txt

4. touch - Create an Empty File

```
touch newfile.txt
```

Creates an empty file named newfile.txt in the current directory.

5. rm - Remove Files or Directories

```
rm newfile.txt
```

Deletes the file newfile.txt.

6. cp - Copy Files or Directories

```
cp file1.txt copy_of_file1.txt
```

Copies file1.txt to copy_of_file1.txt.

7. mv - Move or Rename Files or Directories

```
mv file1.txt renamed_file1.txt
```

Renames file1.txt to renamed_file1.txt.

Understanding Command Options and Arguments:

While running basic commands, it is essential to comprehend how options and arguments enhance functionality:

- Options modify the operation of the command. For instance, the -a option in the ls command:

```
ls -a
```

This lists all files, including hidden ones.

- Arguments specify targets or additional details. In the cp command:

```
cp source_file target_file
```

source_file is the file to be copied, and target_file is the location of the copy.

Combining Multiple Commands:

Often, you may need to run multiple commands in succession. This can be efficiently achieved by chaining commands using operators:

- Semicolon (;) allows consecutive execution:

```
pwd; ls
```

First prints the current directory, then lists the directory contents.

Command Execution with Logical Operators:

- The double ampersand (&&) ensures the second command runs only if the first succeeds:

```
mkdir newdir && cd newdir
```

Creates a directory newdir and changes to it only if creation is successful.

- The double pipe (||) runs the second command only if the first fails:

```
cd nonexistentdir || echo "Directory not found"
```

Attempts to change to nonexistentdir and prints a message if the directory does not exist.

By mastering basic commands, understanding their syntax, and effectively utilizing options and arguments, you lay a solid foundation for advanced Bash scripting and system manipulation. Proficiency in these commands equips you to perform core tasks with efficiency and ease, an indispensable skill for any Bash user.

3.3 Using Command Options and Arguments

In Bash scripting, commands often require additional information to specify precisely what action the command should perform. This additional information is provided through command options and arguments.

Understanding how to use command options and arguments effectively is crucial for writing versatile and powerful Bash scripts.

Command Options are used to modify the behavior of a command. They typically begin with a hyphen (-) or double-hyphen (–) and are followed by one or more letters or words. Short options use a single hyphen followed by a single character, such as -l for long listing format in the ls command. Long options use a double hyphen followed by a word, like –help which displays help information.

Command Arguments are the values or objects that a command acts upon. These can be filenames, directories, or other data that the command processes.

For example, consider the ls command, which lists the contents of a directory. We can enhance its functionality with options and arguments:

```
$ ls -lah /home/user/documents
```

In this example: - ls is the command. - -lah combines three options: - -l lists files in long format. - -a includes hidden files (files starting with a dot). - -h shows file sizes in human-readable format. - /home/user/documents is the argument specifying the directory to list.

Let's break down how options can be combined:

- Short options can be combined into a single command. For example, -lah is a combination of -l, -a, and -h.
- Long options must be specified separately. For example, –all –long –human-readable.

A practical way to understand the use of command options is by reviewing the help system:

```
$ ls --help
```

This command prints out all the available options and their descriptions for the ls command.

For in-depth understanding, let's explore another example using the grep command, which searches for patterns within files. Consider the following command:

```
$ grep -i -r "pattern" /path/to/search
```

Here: - grep is the command. - -i is an option for case-insensitive matching. - -r is an option to search directories recursively. - "pattern" is the argument specifying the search pattern. - /path/to/search is the argument indicating the directory to search in.

To illustrate more complex usage, let's see an example involving the cp command for copying files and directories:

```
$ cp -r -v /source/directory /destination/directory
```

Here: - cp is the command. - -r is an option to copy directories recursively. - -v is an option to enable verbose output, detailing the files being copied. - /source/directory is the argument specifying the source directory. - /destination/directory is the argument specifying the destination directory.

Understanding the importance of command options and arguments becomes clearer when constructing more complex scripts. Consider a script that finds and compresses all log files in a directory:

```
#!/bin/bash
# This script finds all .log files in a directory and compresses them.
find /var/log -name "*.log" -exec gzip {} \;
```

Explanation: - find is the command. - /var/log is the directory to search within. - -name "*.log" is an option-argument pair that filters files ending in .log. - -exec gzip {} specifies that for each found file (represented by {}), gzip is executed to compress the file.

When writing Bash scripts, proper use of command options and arguments can significantly enhance the script's functionality and adaptability. They allow commands to be fine-tuned to perform specific tasks, handle various use cases, and process different input data efficiently.

3.4 Working with Command Aliases

Aliases in Bash scripting are shortcuts for long commands or sequences of commands, allowing for efficiency and reducing repetitive typing. To define an alias, the alias command is used, followed by the name of the alias and the command it represents.

The general syntax for creating an alias is:

```
alias name='command'
```

For example, to create an alias ll for the command ls -l, you would use:

```
alias ll='ls -l'
```

After defining this alias, typing ll in the terminal will execute ls -l. This can significantly save time, especially when dealing with frequently used commands.

It is important to note that aliases are session-specific and will be lost when the terminal session ends. To make an alias permanent, you need to add it to the .bashrc or .bash_profile file located in the user's home directory.

To add an alias to .bashrc, open the file with a text editor:

```
nano ~/.bashrc
```

Append the alias definition to the end of the file, then save and exit the text editor. To ensure the new alias is available in the current session, source the .bashrc file with:

```
source ~/.bashrc
```

Viewing Existing Aliases

To view a list of currently defined aliases, use the alias command with no arguments:

```
alias
```

This will output a list of all aliases currently defined in the session.

Unaliasing

To remove an alias, use the unalias command followed by the alias name:

```
unalias name
```

For example, to remove the ll alias:

```
unalias ll
```

If you need to remove all aliases at once, use:

```
unalias -a
```

Advanced Usage of Aliases

Aliases can also incorporate options and arguments. For instance, creating an alias for rm -i, which prompts before every removal, can prevent accidental deletion of important files:

```
alias rm='rm -i'
```

Moreover, aliases can include complex commands and pipelines. For instance, creating an alias to clean up the tmp directory and then list its contents can be done as follows:

```
alias clean_tmp='rm -rf /tmp/* && ls /tmp'
```

The above example first removes all files and directories in /tmp and then lists the contents of /tmp, verifying the cleanup process.

Alias Limitations

Aliases are limited compared to functions in Bash. They do not support positional parameters and are not parsed by the shell when defined inside scripts. Consequently, for more complex tasks requiring positional parameters or better portability, shell functions are recommended.

```
function lscount {
    echo "Number of files: $(ls -1 | wc -l)"
}
```

Shell functions, unlike aliases, are parsed by the shell and can handle positional parameters, making them suitable for scripts requiring more flexibility.

An alias provides a powerful and convenient way to simplify command execution in everyday Bash operations. For more complex requirements, transitioning from aliases to shell functions ensures better script maintainability and functionality.

3.5 Navigating the Filesystem

In Bash scripting, navigating the filesystem efficiently is crucial for performing file manipulations, executing scripts from different directories, and accessing necessary resources. The Bash shell provides a variety of commands to move around the filesystem and manage files and directories. This section will cover directory navigation commands, directory listings, and essential tools for managing directory contents.

Changing Directories

The cd (change directory) command is used to change the current working directory. The syntax for cd is straightforward:

```
cd [directory]
```

For example, to move to the /home/user/Documents directory, you would use:

```
cd /home/user/Documents
```

To return to the home directory, you can use cd without any arguments or use the tilde (̃) shorthand:

```
cd
\# or
cd ~
```

To navigate to the previous directory, the hyphen (-) can be utilized:

```
cd -
```

Listing Directory Contents

The ls command lists the contents of a directory. Its basic usage is as follows:

```
ls [options] [directory]
```

To list the contents of the current directory:

```
ls
```

Some useful options for ls include:

- -l: Long format listing, showing file permissions, number of links, owner, group, size, and modification time.
- -a: Lists all files, including hidden files (those starting with a dot).
- -h: Human-readable sizes (e.g., 1K, 234M, 2G).
- -R: Recursively lists subdirectories.

Combining these options, you can obtain a comprehensive view of a directory's contents:

```
ls -lahR
```

Current Working Directory

The pwd command (print working directory) displays the current directory's full path:

```
pwd
```

Creating Directories

The mkdir command creates new directories. The basic syntax is:

```
mkdir [options] directoryName
```

To create a new directory named projects:

```
mkdir projects
```

The -p option allows the creation of parent directories as needed:

```
mkdir -p /home/user/new_project/src
```

Removing Directories

Use the rmdir command to remove empty directories:

```
rmdir directoryName
```

To remove the projects directory (if it's empty):

```
rmdir projects
```

For non-empty directories, the rm command with the -r option is used:

```
rm -r directoryName
```

To forcefully remove without prompts, add the -f option:

```
rm -rf projects
```

Copying and Moving Files/Directories

The cp command copies files or directories:

```
cp [options] source destination
```

To copy a file named file.txt to the backup directory:

```
cp file.txt backup/
```

For copying directories, use the -r option:

```
cp -r source_directory destination_directory
```

The mv command moves or renames files or directories:

```
mv [options] source destination
```

To move a file named file.txt to the backup directory:

```
mv file.txt backup/
```

To rename file.txt to file_backup.txt in the same directory:

```
mv file.txt file_backup.txt
```

These commands streamline filesystem navigation and management in Bash, enabling effective handling of directories and files with ease.

3.6 Understanding File Permissions

In Unix-like operating systems, including Linux, each file and directory is assigned specific ownership and permission settings that dictate who can read, write, or execute the file. Understanding and managing these permissions is crucial for system security and effective file management. This section will explore the core concepts of file permissions, the command line tools used to view and modify these settings, and practical examples to illustrate their usage.

Each file has an associated owner and group and a set of permissions divided into three categories: owner permissions, group permissions, and others' permissions. These permissions can be read (r), write (w), and execute (x). The permissions can be viewed using the ls command with the -l option:

```
$ ls -l
```

This command produces an output similar to the following:

```
-rwxr-xr-- 1 user group 4096 Jan 01 12:34 filename
```

From left to right, the columns represent:

- File type and permissions: -rwxr-xr–
- Number of hard links to the file: 1
- Owner of the file: user
- Group of the file: group
- Size of the file in bytes: 4096
- Last modification date and time: Jan 01 12:34
- File name: filename

The first character indicates the type of file (- for regular files, d for directories). The next nine characters are grouped into three sets of three characters each, representing owner, group, and others' permissions, respectively. For example, -rwxr-xr– means:

- Owner permissions: rwx (read, write, execute)
- Group permissions: r-x (read, execute)
- Others' permissions: r– (read)

The chmod command is used to change file permissions. It can be used with symbolic or numeric (octal) mode specifications.

Symbolic Mode

Symbolic mode uses operator characters to modify permissions. The basic syntax is:

```
$ chmod u+r file
$ chmod g-w file
$ chmod o+x file
```

The above commands modify the permissions as follows:

- u+r: Adds read permission for the user (owner).
- g-w: Removes write permission for the group.
- o+x: Adds execute permission for others.

Operators used in symbolic mode are:

- +: Adds a permission.
- -: Removes a permission.
- =: Sets exactly the specified permissions.

Numeric (Octal) Mode

Numeric mode represents permissions with octal numbers. Each permission type is assigned a specific numeric value: read (4), write (2), and execute (1). The permission values for each category (owner, group, others) are summed to create a three-digit octal number:

```
$ chmod 755 file
```

Here, 755 translates to the following permissions:

- Owner: 7 (read + write + execute, 4+2+1 = 7)
- Group: 5 (read + execute, 4+1 = 5)
- Others: 5 (read + execute, 4+1 = 5)

Changing Ownership and Group

File ownership can be modified using the chown command, while group ownership can be changed using the chgrp command:

```
$ sudo chown newuser file
$ sudo chgrp newgroup file
```

The chown command changes the owner of the file to newuser, and the chgrp command changes the group ownership to newgroup. The sudo prefix is often required to modify ownership due to permission restrictions.

```
$ sudo chown newuser:newgroup file
```

This syntax changes both the owner and the group in a single command.

Special Permissions

In addition to the basic read, write, and execute permissions, there are special permissions that can be set using the chmod command:

- setuid (s): When set on an executable, it allows the executable to run with the permissions of the file owner.
- setgid (s): When set on a directory, files created within the directory inherit the group ID.
- sticky bit (t): When set on a directory, only the file owner (or root) can delete or rename files within the directory.

For example, to set the setuid permission:

```
$ chmod u+s file
```

To set the sticky bit on a directory:

```
$ chmod +t directory
```

The above command ensures that only the owner of the directory can delete or rename files within it.

Through understanding and manipulation of file permissions, users can effectively manage access control, thereby enhancing the system security and ensuring that files are shared appropriately.

3.7 Using Wildcards and Globbing

Wildcards are special characters used in Bash scripting to represent one or more characters in file and directory names. These are essential tools for pattern matching and can simplify many tasks by allowing the specification of groups of files or directories without enumerating each explicitly. Globbing is a term that refers to the process of pattern matching using wildcards.

The most common wildcards in Bash are the asterisk (*), the question mark (?), and the square brackets ([]). Each wildcard serves a specific purpose:

- The asterisk (*) matches zero or more characters.
- The question mark (?) matches exactly one character.
- Square brackets ([]) match any one of the enclosed characters.

These wildcards can be used in various Bash commands such as ls, cp, mv, and rm, among others. Their usage enhances the flexibility and power of these commands, making file manipulation efficient.

Using the Asterisk (*)

The asterisk wildcard is used to match zero or more characters. It is useful when you need to select all files of a particular type or those that share a common prefix or suffix.

```
$ ls *.txt
```

This command lists all files in the current directory with a .txt extension.

```
$ rm temp*
```

This command removes all files whose names start with temp, regardless of what follows.

Using the Question Mark (?)

The question mark wildcard matches exactly one character. It is often used when dealing with files that have a common naming pattern but differ slightly.

```
$ ls file?.txt
```

This command lists files named file1.txt, file2.txt, etc., but not file10.txt.

Using Square Brackets ([])

Square brackets allow matching any one of the enclosed characters. It can be used to specify a range of characters or a set of possible characters.

```
$ ls file[123].txt
```

This command lists files named file1.txt, file2.txt, and file3.txt.

Ranges within square brackets are specified using a hyphen (-):

```
$ ls file[a-c].txt
```

This command lists files named filea.txt, fileb.txt, and filec.txt.

Combining Wildcards

Wildcards can be combined in a single command to achieve more complex pattern matching.

```
$ ls *[0-9]?.txt
```

This command lists files that end with one digit followed by any single character and have a .txt extension. Examples include file1a.txt, data2b.txt, etc.

Using Wildcards in Other Commands

Wildcards are not limited to the ls command. They can be used with any command that processes file names including cp, mv, rm, cat, and echo.

For example, to copy all .txt files to another directory, use:

```
$ cp *.txt /path/to/destination/
```

To move all files that start with log and have any single character suffix to the archive directory, use:

```
$ mv log?.txt archive/
```

To concatenate and display the content of all files that have a numerical suffix in their names, use:

```
$ cat file[0-9]*
```

Escaping Wildcards

Sometimes, it is necessary to use the actual characters *, ?, or [] in file names rather than their wildcard function. In such scenarios, escaping these characters with a backslash (\) neutralizes their special meaning.

To list a file literally named data*:

```
$ ls data\*
```

Similarly, to look for a file named example?.txt:

```
$ ls example\?.txt
```

The appropriate use of wildcards, in combination with various Bash commands, allows for powerful file manipulation and automation in scripts. Understanding and effectively employing these tools increase the efficiency and flexibility of script operations in a Unix-like environment.

3.8 Input and Output Redirection

Input and output redirection are fundamental concepts in Bash scripting, enabling the manipulation of data streams to and from commands. These techniques allow for more flexible and efficient handling of input and output without requiring interactive user input or manual output handling.

Standard Streams: Bash utilizes three standard streams: standard input (stdin), standard output (stdout), and standard error (stderr). These streams correspond to file descriptors 0, 1, and 2, respectively.

- stdin (file descriptor 0): This is the default source of input data for a command, typically from the keyboard.
- stdout (file descriptor 1): This is the default destination for output

data from a command, normally displayed on the terminal.

- stderr (file descriptor 2): This is the standard destination for error messages, also usually displayed on the terminal.

Redirecting Standard Output: To redirect standard output to a file, the > operator is used. This will overwrite the contents of the specified file.

```
$ echo "Hello, World!" > output.txt
```

This command redirects the output of the echo command to output.txt. If output.txt does not exist, it is created; if it does exist, its previous content is overwritten.

To append the output to an existing file, the » operator is utilized:

```
$ echo "Append this text." >> output.txt
```

This command appends the string to output.txt instead of overwriting it.

Redirecting Standard Input: Standard input can be redirected from a file using the < operator:

```
$ wc -l < input.txt
```

This command counts the number of lines in input.txt by redirecting the file as input to the wc -l command.

Redirecting Standard Error: To redirect standard error to a file, file descriptor 2 must be specified:

```
$ ls non_existing_file 2> error.log
```

This command attempts to list a non-existing file, redirecting the error message to error.log.

To append error messages to a file, use 2»:

```
$ ls another_missing_file 2>> error.log
```

Redirecting Both Standard Output and Standard Error: In situations where both standard output and error need to be redirected, the &> operator can be used:

```
$ command &> combined_output.txt
```

Alternatively, the following approach directs stdout and stderr to the same file:

```
$ command > output.txt 2>&1
```

Here, standard output is redirected to output.txt, and then standard error is directed to the same file descriptor as standard output.

Here Documents: A here document (or heredoc) is a form of input redirection that allows the inclusion of a block of text within a script. It uses the « operator followed by a delimiter:

```
$ cat << EOF
> This is a here document.
> It allows for multiline input.
> EOF
```

This command sends the text block to the cat command, demonstrating multiline input redirection.

Here Strings: Here strings provide a way to pass a single string to stdin using the «< operator:

```
$ wc -w <<< "Count these words"
```

This command counts the number of words in the provided string.

Combining Redirections: It is possible to combine various redirections for complex command setups. For instance, redirecting stdin from a file, and both stdout and stderr to different files:

```
$ command < input.txt > output.txt 2> error.log
```

Understanding and effectively utilizing input and output redirection techniques are crucial for developing robust and flexible Bash scripts, particularly when automating tasks that involve extensive data handling.

3.9 Piping and Chaining Commands

In Bash scripting, piping and chaining commands are essential techniques for building powerful and efficient command sequences. They allow concatenation of commands and data streams, making complex operations more modular and manageable.

Piping Commands

Piping (‘|‘) is a method for passing the output of one command as input to another. This is particularly useful for processing data in stages, where one command filters or transforms data before passing it to the next. The general syntax for piping is:

```
command1 | command2 | command3
```

For instance, to list directory contents and then search for a specific pattern, you can use:

```
ls -l | grep "pattern"
```

Here, ls -l lists the directory contents in long format, and grep "pattern" filters the output to show only lines containing the specified pattern. We can visualize this pipeline as a series of transformations applied to data flowing through it.

Examples of Piping

- **Using** sort **and** uniq: To sort a list of names and remove duplicate entries:

```
cat names.txt | sort | uniq
```

In this example, cat names.txt reads the names from a file, sort organizes them in alphabetical order, and uniq removes duplicates.

- **Combining** ps **and** grep: To find running processes that match a specific pattern:

```
ps aux | grep "process\_name"
```

ps aux lists all running processes with detailed information, and grep "process_name" filters the list to include only those processes with names matching the pattern.

Chaining Commands

Chaining commands allows the execution of multiple commands in sequence based on logical operators. The primary operators for chaining commands are:

- **Semicolon (';')** : Executes commands sequentially, regardless of the success or failure of preceding commands.

```
command1; command2; command3
```

- **Logical AND ('&&')** : Executes the next command only if the previous command completes successfully (returns a status of 0).

```
command1 && command2 && command3
```

- **Logical OR ('||')** : Executes the next command only if the previous command fails (returns a non-zero status).

```
command1 || command2 || command3
```

Examples of Chaining Commands

- **Using Semicolon (';') and Logical AND ('&&')** : To create a directory and navigate into it if the creation is successful:

```
mkdir new\_dir; cd new\_dir
```

Alternatively, to ensure navigation only if the directory creation succeeds:

```
mkdir new\_dir && cd new\_dir
```

- **Logical OR ('||')** : To attempt changing to a directory and print an error message only if the change fails:

```
cd some\_dir || echo "Failed to change directory."
```

By using chaining commands with logical operators, scripts can make conditional decisions and handle errors gracefully. Combining chaining and piping allows for the creation of sophisticated command sequences that process, filter, and manipulate data efficiently.

3.10 Using Command Substitution

Command substitution enables the output of a command to replace the command itself within a Bash script. This is useful for embedding the output of shell commands within other commands, allowing dynamic command construction and execution. Bash provides two forms of command substitution: using backticks command or the $ syntax.

Consider the following examples of command substitution in practice:

```
current_date=`date`
echo "Today's date is: $current_date"
```

```
Today's date is: Thu Oct 14 10:35:57 UTC 2021
```

In this example, the date command is executed, and its output is stored in the variable current_date. When echo is called, it displays the current date.

Alternatively, the same operation can be performed using the preferable $ syntax, which enhances readability and also allows for nesting:

```
current_date=$(date)
echo "Today's date is: $current_date"
```

```
Today's date is: Thu Oct 14 10:35:57 UTC 2021
```

The $ syntax is more robust and is recommended for most use cases. Consider a more complex scenario where we need to count files in a directory that match a certain pattern:

```
file_count=$(ls *.txt | wc -l)
echo "Number of text files: $file_count"
```

```
Number of text files: 3
```

In this example, the command ls *.txt lists all files with the .txt extension, and wc -l counts the number of lines (files). The result is stored in file_count and subsequently echoed.

Command substitution can be nested to construct more intricate commands. For instance, finding the disk usage of the biggest directory in the current path:

```
largest_dir=$(du -S . | sort -n -r | head -n 1 | awk '{print $2}')
disk_usage=$(du -sh $largest_dir | awk '{print $1}')
echo "The largest directory is: $largest_dir with a usage of: $disk_usage"
```

```
The largest directory is: ./documentation with a usage of: 45M
```

In the above script, multiple commands are chained together. The inner command du -S . | sort -n -r | head -n 1 | awk '{print $2}' determines the largest directory, and the outer command du -sh $largest_dir | awk '{print $1}' calculates its size.

Furthermore, command substitution can capture the output of a command intended for further use or processing. For example, dynamically including the hostname in a filename:

```
backup_file="backup_$(hostname)_$(date +%Y%m%d).tar.gz"
tar -cvzf $backup_file /path/to/directory
```

```
backup_hostname_20211014.tar.gz
```

The backticks method and the $ syntax can both be used for single or multi-line commands. However, for clarity and to avoid errors in complex scripts, the $ method is preferred.

Command substitution is a fundamental technique that offers flexibility and dynamic capabilities in Bash scripting, allowing scripts to be more adaptive and responsive to environment conditions and external outputs. This enhances automation by integrating system state and command outputs seamlessly.

Chapter 4

Working with Variables

This chapter introduces the concept of variables in Bash scripting, explaining how to create, assign, and use them within scripts. It covers variable scope, special variables, and ways to read input into variables. Additionally, readers will learn about manipulating variable content, using arrays, managing environment variables, and parameter expansion, equipping them with essential skills for dynamic scripting.

4.1 Introduction to Variables

In Bash scripting, variables are essential components that store data values, which can be used and manipulated throughout a script. A variable in a Bash script is essentially a pointer to a value that can be referenced, modified, and utilized for various operations. Understanding how to effectively use variables is fundamental for creating dynamic and efficient scripts.

Variables in Bash are typically created by directly assigning a value to a name without any additional keywords, as shown in the following example:

```
variable_name="value"
```

To access the value stored in a variable, prefix the variable name with the dollar sign ($). For example:

```
echo $variable_name
```

This command prints the value of variable_name to the standard output.

Bash variables are by default treated as strings, but they can also hold numeric values. Bash does not require declaring the type of variable explicitly, which contributes to its flexibility. However, it is important to be aware of how variable types are handled, especially when performing arithmetic operations.

```
number=42
echo $number
```

In this example, number is assigned the integer value 42. Strings and integers are treated similarly in variables, but arithmetic evaluations require explicit handling as demonstrated in a later section.

When naming variables, adhere to the following typical conventions:

- Variable names should begin with a letter or an underscore (_).
- Subsequent characters may include letters, digits, or underscores.
- Avoid using special characters such as $, #, %, &, and spaces.
- By convention, environment variables and constants are named using uppercase letters.

Variable names are case-sensitive, meaning VAR and var would be considered distinct. Consider the following example:

```
NAME="Alice"
name="Bob"
echo $NAME
echo $name
```

The output of this script would be:

```
Alice
Bob
```

To include spaces in a variable value, enclose the value in quotes. This ensures that the entire value is treated as a single string.

```
greeting="Hello, world!"
echo $greeting
```

Output:

```
Hello, world!
```

Bash allows for the use of read-only variables that cannot be re-assigned after their initial declaration. This can be achieved using the readonly command, ensuring the variable's immutability throughout the script.

```
readonly PI=3.14159
echo $PI
PI=3.14 # This will generate an error
```

Attempting to re-assign PI would result in an error.

Variables can be exported to ensure they are available to any subprocesses started from the script. The export command performs this task.

```
export PATH="/usr/local/bin:$PATH"
```

This command adds /usr/local/bin to the existing $PATH variable, making it accessible to subprocesses.

There are some special variables in Bash that have predefined meanings and behaviors. For example:

- $0: The name of the script.
- $1, $2, ...: Positional parameters representing arguments passed to the script.
- $$: The process ID of the current shell.
- $!: The process ID of the most recently executed background command.
- $?: The exit status of the last executed command.
- $#: The number of positional parameters.

Understanding these essential aspects of variables is crucial for effective Bash scripting. As we progress, we will delve deeper into advanced topics such as arrays, environment variables, and parameter expansion. These concepts build upon the basics introduced here and empower you to create more complex and functional scripts.

4.2 Creating and Assigning Variables

In Bash scripting, variables are essential for storing data that can be used and manipulated throughout your scripts. Creating and assigning variables are fundamental skills that form the foundation of more complex script operations. Variables in Bash do not require explicit data type declarations; they are dynamically typed, meaning that the type is determined by the context and the content assigned to them.

To create and assign a value to a variable, use the syntax VARIABLE_NAME=VALUE, without any whitespace around the equals sign. Here is an example:

```
#!/bin/bash
# Creating and assigning a simple variable
greeting="Hello, World!"
```

In this example, the variable greeting is assigned the string "Hello, World!". The value can be of any type, including string, integer, or even the result of a command substitution.

Accessing Variable Values

To access the value stored in a variable, precede the variable name with a dollar sign ($). For example, to print the value of the greeting variable, use the following syntax:

```
#!/bin/bash
# Creating and assigning a simple variable
greeting="Hello, World!"

# Accessing and printing the value of the variable
echo $greeting
```

The output of this script would be:

```
Hello, World!
```

Variable Naming Conventions

Bash variable names must follow specific rules:

- Variable names must start with a letter or an underscore character (_).
- They can contain alphanumeric characters and underscores.
- Special characters such as hyphens (-), dollar signs ($), and spaces are not allowed.

Examples of valid variable names are var, Var1, and _var_name. Invalid variable names include 1var, var-name, and var name.

Dynamic Typing and Type Conversion

Bash variables are dynamically typed, which means a variable initially holding a string can be reassigned an integer value without any type conversion issues. Consider the following example:

```
#!/bin/bash
# Assigning a string value
variable="123"

# Reassigning an integer value
variable=456

# Printing the variable value
echo $variable
```

The output will be:

```
456
```

This demonstrates the flexibility of Bash variables.

Command Substitution

Bash allows for the assignment of the output of a command to a variable using command substitution. Enclose the command in the backticks `() or use the $(command) syntax. For example:

```
#!/bin/bash
# Using command substitution to assign the date to a variable
current_date=$(date)
echo "Current date and time: $current_date"
```

The output will display the current date and time as given by the date command:

```
Current date and time: Sun Feb 21 10:10:10 UTC 2023
```

Quoting Variables

Variable values containing spaces or special characters should be enclosed in double quotes. This ensures that the entire value is treated as a single entity. Example:

```
#!/bin/bash
# Assigning a value with spaces
message="Hello, User!"

# Echoing the message without and with quotes
echo $message
echo "$message"
```

Without quotes, the value may be treated as separate words, leading to unexpected results. Properly quoting the variable preserves its integrity.

Exporting Variables

By default, Bash variables are local to the shell in which they are defined. To make a variable available to child processes, use the export command. Example:

```
#!/bin/bash
# Creating an exported variable
export my_var="Exported Variable"

# Calling another script that accesses my_var
./child_script.sh
```

In child_script.sh, the my_var variable will be accessible:

```
#!/bin/bash
# Accessing the exported variable
echo "Value of exported variable: $my_var"
```

This results in:

```
Value of exported variable: Exported Variable
```

Understanding the creation, assignment, and manipulation of variables in Bash is fundamental for developing powerful and flexible scripts that can adapt to various needs. Proper naming conventions, quoting practices, and knowing how and when to export variables further enhance script robustness.

4.3 Using Variables in Scripts

When working with Bash scripts, variables play a significant role in controlling the script's behavior by storing and manipulating data. Before proceeding with more advanced concepts, it is crucial to understand the fundamental operations and syntax for using variables within a script.

Accessing Variables
Once a variable is created and assigned a value, it can be accessed by prefixing the variable name with the dollar sign ($). For example, if we have a variable named var that holds a value, we can reference it in the script as $var to fetch its content.

```
#!/bin/bash
```

```
# Assigning a value to a variable
var="Hello, Bash!"

# Accessing and printing the variable's value
echo $var
```

The output from the above Bash script will be:

```
Hello, Bash!
```

Quoting Variables

Correctly quoting variables is essential to handle spaces and special characters. There are three types of quoting mechanisms in Bash:

- Double quotes: Preserve the spaces and special characters within the quotes but still allow variable expansion.
- Single quotes: Preserve the literal value of each character within the quotes. Variables will not expand.
- Backslash: Escapes a single character.

Consider the following example that illustrates how quoting affects variable expansion and interpretation:

```
#!/bin/bash

# Variable with spaces
var="Hello, Bash!"

# Using double quotes
echo "$var"

# Using single quotes
echo '$var'

# Without quotes
echo $var
```

The output for this script will be:

```
Hello,      Bash!
$var
Hello, Bash!
```

Command Substitution

Bash allows embedding the output of a command as the value of a variable, known as command substitution. This can be done using either backticks (`) or the $() syntax. Here is an example:

```
#!/bin/bash

# Using backticks
```

```
current_date=`date`

# Using $() syntax
current_date_new=$(date)

echo "Current date and time using backticks: $current_date"
echo "Current date and time using $(): $current_date_new"
```

The output will detail the current date and time from the date command:

```
Current date and time using backticks: <current_date>
Current date and time using $(): <current_date>
```

Arithmetic Operations

Unlike many other programming languages, Bash does arithmetic using the let keyword, the ((...)) syntax, or the $((...)) syntax. Here is how you can perform basic arithmetic operations:

```
#!/bin/bash

# Assigning values to variables
num1=10
num2=5

# Using let keyword
let sum=num1+num2
echo "Sum using let: $sum"

# Using double parenthesis
sum=$((num1 + num2))
echo "Sum using double parentheses: $sum"

# Increment and Decrement operations
let num1++
echo "Increment using let: $num1"

num1=$((num1 - 3))
echo "Decrement using double parentheses: $num1"
```

The output from the script will be:

```
Sum using let: 15
Sum using double parentheses: 15
Increment using let: 11
Decrement using double parentheses: 8
```

Using Variables in Strings and Commands

Incorporating variables within strings, commands, and other complex constructs is commonly required in scripts. Here is how variables interact within these contexts:

```
#!/bin/bash

# Defining variables
greeting="Hello"
name="Alice"

# Combining variables in a string
```

```
full_greeting="$greeting, $name!"

# Using variable within a command
directory="myDir"
mkdir "$directory"

echo $full_greeting
echo "Directory $directory created successfully!"
```

The script will output:

```
Hello, Alice!
Directory myDir created successfully!
```

These examples demonstrate the various ways variables can be manipulated in Bash scripts to control program flow and manage data efficiently. Following these approaches, one can effectively use variables to enhance the functionality and flexibility of Bash scripts.

4.4 Understanding Variable Scope

Understanding variable scope is essential for effective Bash scripting. Variable scope determines the visibility and lifespan of variables within a script. There are two primary scopes to consider: local and global. In Bash, the concepts of local and global variables are distinct and necessary for controlling variable access and modifications within various parts of a script.

A global variable is defined outside of any function and is accessible anywhere in the script, including inside functions. By default, all variables are global unless explicitly declared as local. A local variable is restricted to the function in which it is declared and ceases to exist once the function execution is completed.

Global variables can be declared simply by assigning a value to a variable name:

```
# Global variable declaration
global_var="I am global"
```

Since global_var is not confined to any function, it is accessible throughout the script unless redefined inside a function using the local keyword. Here's an example where a global variable is used inside a function:

```
# Function illustrating global variable access
use_global_var() {
    echo "Inside function: $global_var"
}
```

```
# Declare and use the global variable
global_var="I am accessible globally"
echo "Outside function: $global_var"
use_global_var
```

The expected output is:

```
Outside function: I am accessible globally
Inside function: I am accessible globally
```

Local variables, on the other hand, are created using the local keyword within a function. Local variables are not accessible outside the function where they are defined. To declare a local variable within a function:

```
# Function demonstrating local variable scope
local_var_example() {
    local local_var="I am local"
    echo "Inside function: $local_var"
}

# Test the local variable
local_var_example
# Attempt to access local_var outside the function
echo "Outside function: $local_var"
```

This will produce the following output:

```
Inside function: I am local
Outside function:
```

Notice that local_var is not available outside the function, demonstrating the encapsulation provided by local scope.

To understand the implications of variable scope more clearly, consider a scenario where both local and global variables have the same name:

```
# Function with local variable that has the same name as global variable
scope_conflict() {
    local variable="I am local"
    echo "Inside function: $variable"
}

# Define a global variable
variable="I am global"
echo "Outside function (before): $variable"
scope_conflict
echo "Outside function (after): $variable"
```

The output will be:

```
Outside function (before): I am global
Inside function: I am local
Outside function (after): I am global
```

Inside the scope_conflict function, the local variable overrides the global variable with the same name, but outside the function, the global variable remains unaffected. This emphasizes the importance of understanding scope to avoid unintended side effects in script logic.

There are instances when it is crucial to ensure that a variable's value is preserved across different functions or script executions. In such cases, defining variables as global ensures their persistent availability. Conversely, local variables are useful for temporary values that are only relevant within specific functions, minimizing potential conflicts with global variables.

Moreover, variable scope can be thoughtfully leveraged to maintain state and data integrity across function calls and script modules. By using local variables for temporary data within functions and reserving global variables for shared data, scripts can be designed to be more modular and maintainable.

For example, in a larger script that processes user input and updates a global count, the global variable maintains the tally across functions, while local variables handle intermediate computations:

```
# Global count variable
count=0

# Function to increment count
increment_count() {
    local temp_count=$((count + 1))
    count=$temp_count
}

# Increment count thrice
increment_count
increment_count
increment_count

echo "Final count: $count"
```

The script will output:

```
Final count: 3
```

This demonstrates how global variables (count) and local variables (temp_count) can be used together effectively to maintain the desired flow of data and prevent unintended variable overwrites.

By mastering the scope of variables in Bash, scripting becomes more predictable and errors caused by variable conflicts are minimized. This Advanced concept solves complex problems, maintaining robustness and clarity in the code.

4.5 Special Variables

Special variables in Bash scripting are predefined variables that carry specific information about the state of the command shell. These variables are essential for scripts to access information about the environment, user input, and execution status. Special variables typically start with a dollar sign ($) followed by a specific character or a number.

Positional Parameters: Positional parameters are a type of special variables used to reference the arguments passed to a script or function. The first argument is accessed using $1, the second argument using $2, and so on:

```
#!/bin/bash
echo "First argument: $1"
echo "Second argument: $2"
```

Considering the above script is executed with the command ./script.sh arg1 arg2, the output would be:

```
First argument: arg1
Second argument: arg2
```

The special variable $0 represents the name of the script itself. This can be useful for displaying usage instructions or for logging purposes:

```
#!/bin/bash
echo "Script name: $0"
echo "First argument: $1"
```

If you run the script ./script.sh arg1, the output will be:

```
Script name: ./script.sh
First argument: arg1
```

The $* and $@ Variables: Both $* and $@ contain all the positional parameters passed to the script. However, they behave differently when quoted. $* expands to a single string containing all the arguments, whereas $@ expands each argument as a separate string:

```
#!/bin/bash
echo "All arguments with \$*: $*"
echo "All arguments with \$@: $@"

echo "Quoted \$*: \"$*\""
echo "Quoted \$@: \"$@\""
```

Given the command ./script.sh arg1 arg2, the output is:

```
All arguments with $*: arg1 arg2
All arguments with $@: arg1 arg2
Quoted $*: "arg1 arg2"
Quoted $@: "arg1" "arg2"
```

The $# Variable: The special variable $# holds the number of positional parameters provided. This is extremely useful for checking if the user has supplied the correct number of arguments:

```
#!/bin/bash
if [ $# -ne 2 ]; then
  echo "Usage: $0 arg1 arg2"
  exit 1
fi
echo "First argument: $1"
echo "Second argument: $2"
```

When run without arguments or with only one argument, this script will prompt the user with the correct usage:

```
Usage: ./script.sh arg1 arg2
```

More Special Variables:

- $?: Contains the exit status of the last command executed. A value of 0 indicates success, and any non-zero value indicates an error. This can be used to check if the previous command succeeded:

```
#!/bin/bash
mkdir new_directory
if [ $? -eq 0 ]; then
  echo "Directory created successfully."
else
  echo "Failed to create the directory."
fi
```

- $$: Represents the process ID (PID) of the currently executing shell. This can be useful for creating unique filenames or for logging purposes:

```
#!/bin/bash
temp_file="/tmp/tempfile.$$"
echo "Creating temporary file: $temp_file"
touch $temp_file
```

- $!: Stores the process ID of the last background command. This can be used to monitor or control background processes:

```
#!/bin/bash
sleep 60 &
sleep_pid=$!
echo "Started background sleep process with PID: $sleep_pid"
```

- $-: Contains the current options set for the shell. These options can be manipulated using the set command and may influence script behavior:

```
#!/bin/bash
echo "Current shell options: $-"
set -x
echo "Shell options after setting -x: $-"
set +x
```

- $0: Refers to the name of the script or shell. This is particularly useful for displaying usage messages:

```
#!/bin/bash
usage() {
  echo "Usage: $0 [-h] [-f filename]"
}
if [ "$1" == "-h" ]; then
  usage
  exit 0
fi
```

Understanding and utilizing these special variables effectively can significantly enhance the flexibility and functionality of Bash scripts. They provide vital context and control, allowing scripts to interact dynamically with their environment and user inputs.

4.6 Reading Input into Variables

In Bash scripting, one of the fundamental necessities for creating dynamic and interactive scripts is to read input into variables. This allows scripts to gather information from the user or other input sources during runtime, thereby making the scripts adaptable to various contexts and user needs.

The read command is the primary tool in Bash for reading input from standard input (usually the keyboard) and storing it into variables. The basic syntax for using the read command is:

```
read variable_name
```

When the read command is executed, the script pauses and waits for the user to enter input. Once the input is provided and the Enter key is pressed, the input is stored in the specified variable_name. For example:

```
#!/bin/bash
```

```
# Script to read user's name and greet them
echo "Please enter your name:"
read user_name
echo "Hello, $user_name!"
```

Upon running this script, the following interaction occurs:

```
Please enter your name:
John
Hello, John!
```

The read command can also handle multiple variables. When more than one variable name is provided, the input is split into words based on the Internal Field Separator (IFS), and each word is assigned to a corresponding variable. If there are more input words than variable names, the remaining input is assigned to the last variable. Consider the following example:

```
#!/bin/bash
# Script to read first and last name
echo "Please enter your first and last name:"
read first_name last_name
echo "Hello, $first_name $last_name!"
```

The interaction for the above script would be:

```
Please enter your first and last name:
John Doe
Hello, John Doe!
```

The read command offers several useful options. For example, the -p option allows the prompt to be specified directly within the read command, which simplifies the script by combining two commands into one. Here's an example:

```
#!/bin/bash
# Script to read user's name with prompt
read -p "Please enter your name: " user_name
echo "Hello, $user_name!"
```

Additionally, the -s option reads input silently, which is particularly useful for reading sensitive information like passwords. When this option is used, the input is not displayed on the screen:

```
#!/bin/bash
# Script to read a password silently
read -sp "Enter your password: " user_password
echo -e "\nYour password has been recorded."
```

Running the script produces:

```
Enter your password:
Your password has been recorded.
```

Without showing the password input during entry, the read command can dramatically improve security.

Another option is the -t option, which specifies a timeout. read will wait for input for a specified number of seconds; if no input is received within that time, it exits, and the script continues. This can be particularly useful for scripts that should not wait indefinitely for user input:

```
#!/bin/bash
# Script to read input with timeout
if read -t 10 -p "Please enter your name (within 10 seconds): " user_name; then
    echo "Hello, $user_name!"
else
    echo -e "\nTime's up! Proceeding without input."
fi
```

The corresponding interaction could look like:

```
Please enter your name (within 10 seconds):
Time's up! Proceeding without input.
```

Combining the -s and -t options can be applied in scenarios where silent input with a time constraint is required.

One additional feature of the read command is the ability to retrieve input from other file descriptors. This is accomplished using the -u option, which allows a specific file descriptor to be specified. This can be beneficial when dealing with file inputs or other types of input streams.

In a more advanced usage, scripts can capture input from files or command outputs by redirecting the input stream. Here is an example where input is read from a file:

```
#!/bin/bash
# Script to read from a file
while read line; do
    echo "Line: $line"
done < input_file.txt
```

Given an input_file.txt with content:

```
First line of the file
Second line of the file
```

The script output will be:

```
Line: First line of the file
Line: Second line of the file
```

The while loop combined with the read command reads each line of the file into the variable line and processes it.

Mastering input reading into variables using the read command and its various options can greatly enhance the functionality and interactivity of your Bash scripts. Through prudent use of these techniques, scripts can become powerful tools for managing data dynamically and efficiently.

4.7 Manipulating Variable Content

Manipulating the content of variables in Bash scripting is a foundational skill for effective script writing. Bash provides a variety of methods and techniques for performing operations on variables, including string manipulation, arithmetic operations, and built-in commands. This section will explore these methods in detail, allowing you to process data intelligently and dynamically within your scripts.

String Manipulation

String manipulation involves various operations that can be performed on text strings. These operations are often essential for data processing and formatting. Here are some common string manipulation techniques:

- Concatenation: Concatenating, or combining, two or more strings.
- Substring Extraction: Extracting a portion of a string.
- Length of String: Determining the length of a string.
- Replacing Substrings: Replacing occurrences of a substring within a string.
- Changing Case: Converting strings to upper or lower case.

Concatenation

String concatenation can be done using simple syntax where the two strings are placed side by side:

```
first_string="Hello"
second_string="World"
combined_string="${first_string} ${second_string}"
echo ${combined_string}
```

```
Hello World
```

Substring Extraction

Substring extraction allows for retrieving a portion of a string. The general syntax is $variable:offset:length:

```
full_string="Bash is powerful"
substring=${full_string:5:2}
echo ${substring}
```

is

Length of String

To find the length of a string, use the syntax $#variable:

```
string="Length"
length=${#string}
echo ${length}
```

6

Replacing Substrings

Replacing a substring within a string can be achieved using pattern matching syntax $variable//search/replace:

```
original_string="I have a cat"
modified_string=${original_string//cat/dog}
echo ${modified_string}
```

I have a dog

Changing Case

Changing the case of letters in a string uses built-in commands:

```
string="Case Change"
lowercase_string=${string,,}
uppercase_string=${string^^}
echo ${lowercase_string} # outputs: case change
echo ${uppercase_string} # outputs: CASE CHANGE
```

case change
CASE CHANGE

Arithmetic Operations

Bash can perform arithmetic operations using the expr command or double-parentheses syntax:

- Addition: result=$((a + b))
- Subtraction: result=$((a - b))
- Multiplication: result=$((a * b))
- Division: result=$((a / b))

Using the double-parentheses syntax:

```
a=10
b=5
sum=$((a + b))
difference=$((a - b))
product=$((a * b))
quotient=$((a / b))

echo "Sum: $sum"
echo "Difference: $difference"
echo "Product: $product"
echo "Quotient: $quotient"
```

```
Sum: 15
Difference: 5
Product: 50
Quotient: 2
```

The expr command can also be used, although it is less preferred for its verbosity and requirement for backticks or the $( ) syntax to capture results:

```
result=$(expr 5 + 2)
echo ${result}
```

```
7
```

Parameter Expansion

Parameter expansion provides advanced ways to manipulate the content of variables. This includes default values, substring replacement, and more. Key techniques include:

- Default Value: Using $variable:-default to provide a default value.
- Substitution: String substitution within a variable using $variable/-pattern/replacement.
- Substring: Extracting a substring using $variable:offset:length as mentioned earlier.

For example, using a default value:

```
: ${my_variable:=default_value}
echo ${my_variable}
```

```
default_value
```

String substitution within a variable:

```
filename="document.txt"
new_filename=${filename/.txt/.pdf}
echo ${new_filename}
```

document.pdf

By mastering these variable manipulation techniques, you can write more powerful and flexible Bash scripts. These methods enable precise control over data, streamline processing, and enhance the capabilities of your scripts within the realm of shell scripting.

4.8 Using Arrays in Bash

Arrays in Bash offer a powerful means to manage collections of values. Unlike some programming languages, arrays do not hold to a strict size in Bash; their size gets determined dynamically. An array index can begin with zero and continue to any positive integer. This section addresses how to define arrays, access their elements, iterate through them, and leverage associative arrays for more complex indexing with string keys.

Defining an array is straightforward. Using parentheses, one can initialize an array with elements separated by spaces:

```
fruits=('apple' 'banana' 'cherry' 'date')
```

Accessing individual elements within an array necessitates the usage of the index and the $ symbol with braces, as shown:

```
echo ${fruits[1]}
```

This line will output banana as it corresponds to the second element in the array (indices start at zero).

To retrieve all elements of the array, use:

```
echo ${fruits[@]}
# or
echo ${fruits[*]}
```

Both $fruits[@] and $fruits[*] will output the contents: apple banana cherry date.

Appending elements to an existing array is feasible by specifying a new index:

```
fruits[4]='elderberry'
```

The array fruits now contains five elements. The array can be processed element by element using loops. A for loop, for instance, accesses each array element:

```
for fruit in "${fruits[@]}"; do
  echo "$fruit"
done
```

Execution of the above code will print each fruit on a separate line. Arrays also support numeric indexing via parameter expansion. It is useful for iterating with explicit indices:

```
for i in "${!fruits[@]}"; do
  echo "Index $i contains ${fruits[$i]}"
done
```

The ! symbol used here with an array returns the indices. Therefore, the above loop not only accesses the value but also specifies its position in the array.

Bash also supports associative arrays that allow string indices. However, one must declare an associative array with declare -A:

```
declare -A colors
colors[apple]='green'
colors[banana]='yellow'
colors[cherry]='red'
```

Accessing and iterating through associative arrays follows a pattern similar to indexed arrays, though using string indices:

```
echo ${colors[banana]} # outputs 'yellow'

for key in "${!colors[@]}"; do
  echo "The color of $key is ${colors[$key]}"
done
```

This prints:

```
The color of apple is green
The color of banana is yellow
The color of cherry is red
```

Enumerating the length of an array employs the built-in # symbol:

```
num_fruits=${#fruits[@]}
echo "The number of fruits is $num_fruits"
```

Thus, an output of 5 represents the total number of elements in the array.

Dynamic manipulation of arrays often involves removing elements. Unsetting an element utilizes the unset command:

```
unset fruits[2]
```

Following the removal, fruits will no longer contain the element at index 2.

Array slicing in Bash offers partial retrieval of array contents using a specified range. The notation $array[@]:start:length defines the starting element and the length of the slice:

```
echo ${fruits[@]:1:2} # outputs 'banana date'
```

In scripting, managing arrays efficiently necessitates awareness of such array manipulation actions. For a more complex and dynamic script behavior, understanding these array operations provides an essential skill set.

4.9 Environment Variables

Environment variables play a crucial role in the configuration and operation of Bash scripts. These variables are accessible across different sessions and programs, making them vital for system-wide settings and user preferences. Understanding how to utilize environment variables effectively will empower you to create more dynamic and adaptable scripts.

Environment variables are typically uppercase, by convention, to distinguish them from regular shell variables. Common environment variables include HOME, PATH, USER, and SHELL. These variables provide information about the current user's environment and system configuration.

To list all environment variables and their values, you can use the env command:

```
env
```

You can also print the value of a specific environment variable using the echo command:

```
echo $HOME
echo $PATH
```

To set an environment variable in Bash, use the export command. This makes the variable available to all child processes started from the current shell. For example:

```
export MY_VARIABLE="Hello, World!"
```

This variable can now be accessed by any script or command launched from the same shell. To verify that the environment variable has been set, you can use the echo command:

```
echo $MY_VARIABLE
```

Consider the following example where we use an environment variable within a script. Create a file named example.sh and include the following code:

```
#!/bin/bash

echo "The value of MY_VARIABLE is: $MY_VARIABLE"
```

Make the script executable:

```
chmod +x example.sh
```

Run the script:

```
./example.sh
```

If MY_VARIABLE is set in the environment, the script will print its value. To ensure that a script sets an environment variable only for its duration, you can place the export statement within the script:

```
#!/bin/bash

export TEMP_VARIABLE="Temp Value"
echo "The value of TEMP_VARIABLE is: $TEMP_VARIABLE"
```

After the script execution, TEMP_VARIABLE will not persist in the environment of the parent shell.

To unset an environment variable, use the unset command:

```
unset MY_VARIABLE
```

It is prudent to understand the implications of modifying critical environment variables. For instance, modifying the PATH variable can affect the system's ability to locate executables. Here is how you can append a directory to the PATH variable:

```
export PATH=$PATH:/new/directory
```

The .profile, .bash_profile, and .bashrc files in the user's home directory are commonly used to set environment variables permanently. For instance, adding the following lines to .bashrc adds a new directory to the PATH variable each time a new shell session starts:

```
# Add custom directory to PATH
export PATH=$PATH:/new/directory
```

After modifying .bashrc, reload it to apply the changes without restarting the session:

```
source ~/.bashrc
```

Environment variables can also be classified into two categories: user-specific and system-wide. User-specific environment variables are defined in files like .bashrc or .bash_profile, while system-wide environment variables are defined in /etc/environment, /etc/profile, or /etc/bash.bashrc. Changes to system-wide environment variables affect all users and hence require administrative privileges.

Here is an example of defining a system-wide environment variable. Append the following line to /etc/environment:

```
/etc/environment:
MY_GLOBAL_VAR="Global Value"
```

Environment variables are equally essential when scripting for different environments or deploying applications. They permit seamless configuration adjustments without altering the underlying code. This capability is particularly beneficial in software development workflows and continuous integration/continuous deployment (CI/CD) pipelines.

Understanding environment variables enhances your ability to configure and control your scripting environment efficiently. Being meticulous with variable naming and cautious with critical variables helps maintain a stable and predictable system performance.

4.10 Parameter Expansion

Parameter expansion is a fundamental aspect of Bash scripting that allows you to manipulate the values of variables. This feature enables more flexible and dynamic scripts by providing mechanisms to modify and use variable data in various ways. In this section, we explore the syntax and applications of parameter expansion, covering techniques such as default values, substring extraction, pattern matching, and indirect expansion.

Default Values

Default values can be specified for variables that may not have been initialized. This ensures that scripts behave predictably even when some variables are not set. Bash uses the following syntax for default values:

```
${variable:-default_value}
```

In this example, default_value is returned if variable is unset or null. Otherwise, the value of variable is returned. Consider the following script:

```
#!/bin/bash
name=${1:-"Guest"}
echo "Hello, $name!"
```

When executed without an argument, the output will be:

```
Hello, Guest!
```

If an argument is provided, the output will reflect the supplied value:

```
Hello, Alice!
```

Substring Extraction

Parameter expansion also supports substring extraction, which allows you to extract a portion of a string. The syntax for substring extraction is:

```
${variable:offset:length}
```

Here, offset specifies the starting position, and length defines the number of characters to extract. If length is omitted, the substring extends to the end of the string. For example:

```
text="Bash scripting"
subtext=${text:5:9}
echo $subtext
```

The output will be:

```
scripting
```

Substring Replacement

Bash allows for the replacement of substrings within a variable. This can be useful for altering variable values without creating new ones. The general form for substring replacement is:

```
${variable//search/replace}
```

This replaces all occurrences of search with replace. To replace only the first occurrence, use a single forward slash:

```
text="The quick brown fox"
new_text=${text/quick/slow}
echo $new_text
```

The output will be:

```
The slow brown fox
```

To replace all occurrences:

```
new_text=${text//o/x}
echo $new_text
```

The output will change to:

```
The quick brxwn fx
```

Pattern Matching

Pattern matching is a powerful Bash feature that allows complex string manipulations. There are special characters such as *, ?, and [ ] which act as wildcards. Consider the following example for removing a pattern from the beginning or end of a variable:

```
file="archive.tar.gz"
basename=${file%.tar.gz}
echo $basename
```

The output will be:

```
archive
```

In this case, %.tar.gz indicates that the suffix .tar.gz should be removed from file. Similarly, % can be used for suffix removal, and # for prefix removal:

```
filepath="/home/user/docs/file.txt"
filename=${filepath##*/}
echo $filename
```

The command removes the longest match of the pattern */ from the beginning, yielding:

file.txt

Indirect Expansion

Indirect expansion lets you reference the value of a variable whose name is stored in another variable. This is particularly useful in dynamic scripts where variable names are determined at runtime. The syntax for indirect expansion is:

```
ref="var"
var="value"
echo ${!ref}
```

Here, $!ref evaluates to the value stored in var, resulting in the output:

value

Length of Variable

Bash allows you to determine the length of a variable's value using the following syntax:

```
${#variable}
```

For example:

```
text="Bash scripting"
length=${#text}
echo $length
```

The output will be:

14

Understanding and utilizing parameter expansion effectively can greatly enhance the robustness and flexibility of your Bash scripts, providing powerful tools for variable manipulation and string operations.

Chapter 5

Control Structures

This chapter explores control structures in Bash scripting, including conditional statements (if, elif, else), logical operators, and the case statement. It covers various loops (for, while, until), break and continue statements, and using select for creating menus. The chapter also discusses nesting control structures, writing complex conditions, and handling errors and exit statuses to create more dynamic and efficient scripts.

5.1 Introduction to Control Structures

In Bash scripting, control structures are fundamental constructs that determine the flow and logic of the script execution. They enable the scripting environment to make decisions, repeat certain actions, and select between different options based on given conditions. The mastery of control structures is crucial for writing efficient, dynamic, and robust scripts.

Control structures in Bash can be broadly categorized into conditional statements, loops, and branching mechanisms. Each category serves a distinct purpose and can be combined to achieve complex script functionalities. This section provides an overview of these core constructs, laying the groundwork for detailed exploration in subsequent sections.

The primary control structures covered in this chapter include:

- **Conditional Statements:** These include if, elif, and else, which are used to execute commands based on specific conditions.

- **Logical Operators:** Operators such as &&, ||, and ! which enable the conjunction, disjunction, and negation of conditions.
- **Case Statement:** This provides a mechanism to select from multiple possible execution paths based on the value of a variable or an expression.
- **Loops:** Constructs like for, while, and until that allow for repetitive execution of commands.
- **Break and Continue Statements:** These are used to control loop execution by breaking out of the loop or skipping to the next iteration.
- **Select for Menus:** A special loop that creates a simple menu from which the user can choose options.

Each control structure is tailored to address specific scripting needs, and choosing the right construct depends on the task at hand. Understanding the syntax and behavior of these constructs is essential for leveraging their full potential.

Consider a scenario in which a script must verify whether a directory exists and create it if it does not. Using an if statement, this verification can be incorporated as follows:

```
directory="mydir"

if [ ! -d "$directory" ]; then
  mkdir "$directory"
  echo "Directory created."
else
  echo "Directory already exists."
fi
```

In this script, the if statement checks if the directory does not exist ([! -d "$directory"]). If the condition is true, it creates the directory and prints a confirmation message. Otherwise, it simply notes that the directory already exists. The syntax of the condition inside square brackets ([ ]) is critical: -d tests for directory existence, and the exclamation mark (!) negates the condition.

Looping constructs, on the other hand, enable the automation of repetitive tasks. For example, a for loop can be employed to iterate over a list of files and perform operations on each:

```
for file in *.txt; do
  cat "$file" >> combined.txt
done
```

In this example, the for loop iterates over all .txt files in the current directory, concatenating their contents into a single file called combined.txt. The construct for variable in list; do commands; done is intrinsic to the for loop's functionality.

The versatility of control structures extends beyond simple expressions and loops. Bash scripting supports the use of more sophisticated logic through nested control structures and complex conditions. Nesting involves placing one control structure inside another, enabling the construction of multifaceted logic. Complex conditions, utilizing multiple logical operators, facilitate the execution of commands based on intricate criteria.

For instance, imagine a scenario requiring a program to check multiple conditions before executing a command:

```
if [ -x "$file" ] && [ "$USER" = "admin" ]; then
  echo "File is executable and user is admin."
else
  echo "Condition not met."
fi
```

In this example, the if statement evaluates two conditions combined with the logical AND operator (&&): whether the file is executable (-x "$file") and whether the current user is admin ("$USER" = "admin"). If both conditions are met, the script outputs a confirmation message; otherwise, it notes that the condition is not met.

Grasping control structures in Bash scripting inherently involves practice and experimentation. Through systematic exploration and application of these constructs, a proficient understanding will be attained, empowering the creation of dynamic and efficient scripts.

5.2 Conditional Statements: if, elif, else

In Bash scripting, conditional statements allow the execution of commands based on the evaluation of conditions. These conditions typically compare variables or check the status of commands, enabling decision-making processes within the script. The primary conditional control structure in Bash includes if, elif, and else statements.

The if statement evaluates a condition and executes a block of code if the condition is true. The syntax of the if statement is as follows:

```
if [ condition ]
then
    # Commands to execute if condition is true
fi
```

The condition is enclosed within brackets [ ] and can include various operators to compare numbers, strings, or file statuses. For example, to check if a variable x is equal to 5:

```
x=5
if [ \$x -eq 5 ]
then
    echo "x is 5"
fi
```

When the condition within the brackets evaluates to true, the block of commands between then and fi is executed. If the condition is false, the block is skipped.

To handle multiple conditions, if statements can be extended using elif (else if) and else clauses. The syntax incorporating elif and else is:

```
if [ condition1 ]
then
    # Commands to execute if condition1 is true
elif [ condition2 ]
then
    # Commands to execute if condition2 is true
else
    # Commands to execute if none of the above conditions are true
fi
```

Each elif condition is evaluated sequentially, and the corresponding block of code is executed if the condition is true. If none of the conditions are met, the else block is executed. For instance:

```
x=5
if [ \$x -eq 1 ]
then
    echo "x is 1"
elif [ \$x -eq 5 ]
then
    echo "x is 5"
else
    echo "x is neither 1 nor 5"
fi
```

In this example, the script prints x is 5 because the second condition is true.

Bash provides several operators for comparison in conditional statements. Some commonly used numerical comparison operators include:

- -eq: Equal to
- -ne: Not equal to
- -lt: Less than
- -le: Less than or equal to
- -gt: Greater than
- -ge: Greater than or equal to

For string comparisons, the following operators are used:

- =: Equal to
- !=: Not equal to
- -z string: True if the string length is zero
- -n string: True if the string length is non-zero

Consider a script that checks for user-provided input and acts accordingly:

```
read -p "Enter your name: " name
if [ -z "\$name" ]
then
    echo "No name entered"
elif [ "\$name" = "Alice" ]
then
    echo "Hello, Alice!"
else
    echo "Nice to meet you, \$name!"
fi
```

In this script, the user inputs their name. The if statement first checks if the name variable is empty (zero length) using the -z operator. If true, it prints No name entered. If the name is Alice, it prints a personalized greeting. For any other input, it greets the user with their entered name.

Beyond straightforward comparisons, conditional statements in Bash also support logical operators to combine multiple conditions. The logical operators include:

- [condition1 -a condition2]: Logical AND

- [condition1 -o condition2]: Logical OR
- [! condition]: Logical NOT

For instance, consider a script to check if a file exists and is not empty:

```
file="myfile.txt"
if [ -f "\$file" ] && [ -s "\$file" ]
then
    echo "File exists and is not empty"
else
    echo "File does not exist or is empty"
fi
```

Here, -f $file checks if the file exists, and -s $file checks if the file size is greater than zero. The && operator ensures both conditions must be true for the then block to execute.

Through mastery of if, elif, and else statements, combined with comparing numerical values, strings, and logical conditions, one can create flexible and dynamic Bash scripts to automate a wide array of tasks efficiently.

5.3 Using Logical Operators

Logical operators are essential in Bash scripting as they facilitate complex condition evaluations. These operators allow combining multiple conditions within a single conditional statement. In Bash, the primary logical operators are && (logical AND), || (logical OR), and the unary ! (logical NOT).

Logical AND Operator (&&): The logical AND operator && allows executing a subsequent command only if the preceding command returns a zero exit status (success). When used within an if statement, it enables multiple conditions to be true simultaneously.

Example:

```
#!/bin/bash
# Check both conditions: if directory exists and file exists within that directory

if [ -d "/home/user" ] && [ -f "/home/user/.bashrc" ]; then
    echo "Directory exists and the file is present."
else
    echo "Either directory does not exist or the file is absent."
fi
```

In this script, the if statement checks both conditions:

- Whether the directory /home/user exists.
- Whether the file /home/user/.bashrc exists.

Both conditions must satisfy to execute the first echo statement. If either condition fails, the script proceeds to the else block.

Logical OR Operator (||): The logical OR operator || executes a subsequent command if the preceding command returns a non-zero exit status (failure). Within an if statement, it enables execution when at least one condition is true.

Example:

```
#!/bin/bash
# Check any condition: if the disk usage is above 90% or swap usage is above 90%

disk_usage=$(df / | grep / | awk '{print $5}' | sed 's/%//')
swap_usage=$(free | grep Swap | awk '{print $3/$2 * 100.0}')

if [ $disk_usage -gt 90 ] || [ $swap_usage -gt 90 ]; then
    echo "Warning: Disk or Swap usage is above 90%."
else
    echo "Disk and Swap usage are within safe limits."
fi
```

In this script:

- disk_usage is obtained using the df command, which reports file system disk space usage.
- swap_usage calculated by the free command shows the swap memory usage.

If either condition (disk_usage > 90 or swap_usage > 90) satisfies, the echo statement within the if block executes. Otherwise, the script proceeds to the else block.

Logical NOT Operator (!): The logical NOT operator ! inverts the exit status of a command or condition. It is useful for conditions where you need to check if a particular command or condition fails.

Example:

```
#!/bin/bash
# Check if a user does not exist on the system

username="newuser"

if ! id -u "$username" > /dev/null 2>&1; then
    echo "User $username does not exist."
else
```

```
    echo "User $username exists."
fi
```

In this script:

- id -u "$username" checks if a user with username exists on the system.
- The output is redirected to null device /dev/null to suppress it.

If the user does not exist, the script executes the command within the if block. If the user exists, the script executes the else block command.

Combining Logical Operators: Bash allows combining multiple logical operators to form complex conditions. Parentheses can group conditions and specify order precedence.

Example:

```
#!/bin/bash
# Complex conditions with logical operators

mem_usage=$(free | grep Mem | awk '{print $3/$2 * 100.0}')
load_average=$(cat /proc/loadavg | awk '{print $1}')

if [ $(echo "$mem_usage > 80" | bc) -eq 1 ] && [ $(echo "$load_average < 1.0" | bc) -
    eq 1 ] || [ -f "/var/log/syslog" ]; then
    echo "High memory usage and low load OR syslog file exists."
else
    echo "Condition not met."
fi
```

This script:

- Checks if mem_usage is greater than 80% and load_average is less than 1.0 or if /var/log/syslog file exists.
- Uses bc for floating-point comparison.

Seamlessly combining these logical operators facilitates intricate condition checks and decision-making processes within Bash scripts. Logical operators enhance the robustness and control of script execution paths in complex environments.

5.4 The Case Statement

The case statement provides a convenient solution to handle multiple conditional branches. It simplifies complex if-elif-else ladders by categorizing and executing commands based on different patterns of a given expression. This structure is valuable when checking a variable against a set of values, enabling streamlined and readable code.

The basic syntax of the case statement is as follows:

```
case $variable in
  pattern1)
    commands
    ;;
  pattern2)
    commands
    ;;
  pattern3|pattern4)
    commands
    ;;
  *)
    default_commands
    ;;
esac
```

Here, $variable is evaluated against multiple patterns. The commands associated with the first matching pattern are executed. Patterns are defined according to shell pattern matching rules which can include wildcards and alternations. Each pattern block ends with a double semicolon ;;, and the default case, optional but often useful, is specified with * to handle unmatched patterns.

Consider the following practical example where we use the case statement to handle user input for selecting a day of the week:

```
#!/bin/bash

echo "Enter a day of the week:"
read day

case $day in
  "Monday")
    echo "Start of the work week."
    ;;
  "Tuesday")
    echo "Second day of the work week."
    ;;
  "Wednesday")
    echo "Midweek day."
    ;;
  "Thursday")
    echo "Just one more day to Friday."
    ;;
  "Friday")
    echo "Last work day of the week."
    ;;
  "Saturday"|"Sunday")
    echo "Weekend!"
    ;;
  *)
    echo "Invalid input. Please enter a valid day of the week."
```

```
    ;;
esac
```

In this example, based on the user's input stored in $day, the case statement checks each provided pattern. When a match is found, the corresponding echo command is executed. For days matching "Saturday" or "Sunday," a single echo command outputs "Weekend!".

Combining Patterns and Wildcards

The case statement can also manage multiple patterns within a single clause using pipe | (alternation) or handle complex matches with wildcard characters.

Consider the scenario where we manage file types based on extensions:

```
#!/bin/bash

echo "Enter a filename:"
read filename

case $filename in
  *.txt)
    echo "Text file"
    ;;
  *.jpg|*.png|*.gif)
    echo "Image file"
    ;;
  *.tar.gz|*.zip)
    echo "Compressed file"
    ;;
  *)
    echo "Unknown file type"
    ;;
esac
```

Here, the patterns include wildcards such as *.txt for text files, image file extensions *.jpg | *.png | *.gif, and compressed file formats *.tar.gz | *.zip. The case statement executes commands based on the file extension provided by the user.

Handling Positional Parameters

Another powerful application of the case statement is managing script parameters. Let's examine a script that processes command-line options:

```
#!/bin/bash

case $1 in
  start)
    echo "Starting the service..."
    ;;
  stop)
```

```
    echo "Stopping the service..."
    ;;
  restart)
    echo "Restarting the service..."
    ;;
  status)
    echo "The service status is: active"
    ;;
  *)
    echo "Usage: $0 {start|stop|restart|status}"
    ;;
esac
```

In this example, $1 references the first positional parameter provided to the script. Based on this parameter, the case statement determines the command to execute. If no valid option is provided, the default case outputs a usage message.

Nesting Case Statements for Advanced Conditions

Although less common, nesting case statements within one another enables handling more complex conditions. Here is an example illustrating nested case statements to manage a more advanced set of conditions concerning a meal order:

```
#!/bin/bash

echo "Select a meal type (breakfast, lunch, dinner):"
read meal

case $meal in
  "breakfast")
    echo "Select a breakfast item (pancakes, waffles, cereal):"
    read item
    case $item in
      "pancakes")
        echo "You chose pancakes."
        ;;
      "waffles")
        echo "You chose waffles."
        ;;
      "cereal")
        echo "You chose cereal."
        ;;
      *)
        echo "Invalid breakfast item."
        ;;
    esac
    ;;
  "lunch"|"dinner")
    echo "Select a main course (pizza, burger, salad):"
    read main
    case $main in
      "pizza")
        echo "You chose pizza."
        ;;
      "burger")
        echo "You chose burger."
```

```
            ;;
        "salad")
            echo "You chose salad."
            ;;
        *)
            echo "Invalid main course."
            ;;
    esac
    ;;
  *)
    echo "Invalid meal type."
    ;;
esac
```

In this script, based on the user's input for meal, a second case statement is invoked to handle specific options related to that meal. Nested case statements can greatly enhance script functionality by allowing more detailed and contextual handling of conditions.

Integrating the case statement into scripts not only improves readability but also allows structured and efficient management of multiple conditional paths. This control structure's flexibility, from matching simple strings to incorporating wildcards and nested logic, makes it a fundamental tool in proficient Bash scripting.

5.5 Loops: for, while, until

Loops are a fundamental aspect of programming that allow the execution of a set of instructions repeatedly until a certain condition is met. In Bash scripting, the for, while, and until loops provide powerful and flexible constructs for iteration. Understanding and effectively using these loops can greatly enhance the efficiency and readability of your scripts.

The for loop: The for loop iterates over a list of items, executing the commands within the loop body for each item. The syntax for a basic for loop is as follows:

```
for variable in list
do
    commands
done
```

In this structure, variable takes on the value of each item in list in turn, and the commands within the do block are executed for each value of variable. Here is an example of a for loop that prints numbers from 1 to 5:

```
for i in 1 2 3 4 5
do
    echo "Number: $i"
done
```

The output of the above script will be:

```
Number: 1
Number: 2
Number: 3
Number: 4
Number: 5
```

The for loop can also iterate over the output of a command, such as the contents of a directory:

```
for file in $(ls)
do
    echo "File: $file"
done
```

This script will list all files in the current directory.

The while **loop:** The while loop continues to execute as long as its condition evaluates to true. The general syntax of a while loop is:

```
while condition
do
    commands
done
```

Here, condition is tested before each iteration of the commands inside the loop. An example of a while loop that prints numbers from 1 to 5 is:

```
i=1
while [ $i -le 5 ]
do
    echo "Number: $i"
    i=$((i + 1))
done
```

The output will be:

```
Number: 1
Number: 2
Number: 3
Number: 4
Number: 5
```

In this example, the loop continues until i exceeds 5. Note the use of the arithmetic evaluation syntax $((...)) to increment the value of i.

The until loop: The until loop is similar to the while loop, but it continues to execute as long as its condition evaluates to false. The syntax for an until loop is:

```
until condition
do
    commands
done
```

Here's an example of an until loop that prints numbers from 1 to 5:

```
i=1
until [ $i -gt 5 ]
do
    echo "Number: $i"
    i=$((i + 1))
done
```

The output is the same as previous examples:

```
Number: 1
Number: 2
Number: 3
Number: 4
Number: 5
```

In this script, the loop runs as long as i is not greater than 5.

Nested Loops: Loops can be nested within each other, allowing for more complex iterations. Here is an example of a for loop nested inside another for loop:

```
for i in 1 2 3
do
    for j in a b c
    do
        echo "Combination: $i$j"
    done
done
```

The output will be:

```
Combination: 1a
Combination: 1b
Combination: 1c
Combination: 2a
Combination: 2b
Combination: 2c
Combination: 3a
Combination: 3b
Combination: 3c
```

This nested loop structure iterates over all combinations of the elements in the two lists.

Using Loop Control Statements: The break and continue statements can control the flow of a loop. The break statement exits the loop entirely, while the continue statement skips the remainder of the loop body and proceeds to the next iteration. Here is an example of using break:

```
for i in 1 2 3 4 5
do
    if [ $i -eq 3 ]
    then
        break
    fi
    echo "Number: $i"
done
```

The output will be:

```
Number: 1
Number: 2
```

As soon as i equals 3, the break statement exits the loop.

Using continue works in a similar fashion:

```
for i in 1 2 3 4 5
do
    if [ $i -eq 3 ]
    then
        continue
    fi
    echo "Number: $i"
done
```

The output will show numbers excluding 3:

```
Number: 1
Number: 2
Number: 4
Number: 5
```

Practical Examples: The following practical example demonstrates downloading files from a list of URLs using the for loop:

```
urls="http://example.com/file1 http://example.com/file2 http://example.com/file3"
for url in $urls
do
    wget $url
done
```

In a real scenario, to avoid being blocked by some servers, you might want to introduce a delay between downloads. You can achieve this by using the sleep command:

```
urls="http://example.com/file1 http://example.com/file2 http://example.com/file3"
```

```
for url in $urls
do
    wget $url
    sleep 5
done
```

This variation of the script pauses for 5 seconds between downloads.

Another practical example is processing lines from a file using a while loop with read:

```
while IFS= read -r line
do
    echo "Processing: $line"
done < inputfile.txt
```

The while loop reads each line from inputfile.txt and processes it.

Combining loops with user interaction can create dynamic and interactive scripts. The following example prompts the user to enter names until they decide to stop:

```
names=()
while true
do
    read -p "Enter a name (or type 'quit' to stop): " name
    if [ "$name" == "quit" ]
    then
        break
    fi
    names+=("$name")
done

echo "Names entered: ${names[@]}"
```

This script collects names until the user types 'quit', and then displays all entered names.

Understanding and effectively using for, while, and until loops allows for writing powerful and efficient Bash scripts. These constructs are essential for automating repetitive tasks and can handle various scenarios in complex scripting tasks.

5.6 Break and Continue Statements

The break and continue statements are essential tools in Bash scripting, providing control over the flow of loops in a script. Understanding and correctly implementing these statements can greatly increase the efficiency and readability of your code. Below, we will delve into each statement, its syntax, and its practical applications.

The break statement is used to exit from a loop prematurely. This can be particularly useful when a certain condition warrants an early termination of the loop. Here's a basic example of the break statement within a while loop:

```
#!/bin/bash

counter=1
while [ $counter -le 10 ]; do
  echo "Iteration $counter"
  if [ $counter -eq 5 ]; then
    break
  fi
  ((counter++))
done
```

In this script, the loop runs until counter exceeds 10, but it includes a condition that checks if counter equals 5. When this condition is met, the break statement is executed, exiting the loop immediately. Thus, the output of the script will be:

```
Iteration 1
Iteration 2
Iteration 3
Iteration 4
Iteration 5
```

The continue statement, on the other hand, is used to skip the remainder of the current loop iteration and jump to the next iteration. This can be useful for skipping specific values or iterations based on certain conditions. Below is an example using the continue statement in a for loop:

```
#!/bin/bash

for number in {1..10}; do
  if [ $number -eq 5 ]; then
    continue
  fi
  echo "Number: $number"
done
```

Here, when number equals 5, the continue statement is executed, causing the script to skip that iteration and proceed with the next value. The output of this script will be:

```
Number: 1
Number: 2
Number: 3
Number: 4
Number: 6
Number: 7
Number: 8
Number: 9
Number: 10
```

When using break and continue in nested loops, you can further control the depth of the exit or continuation by specifying a numerical argument. By default, break and continue affect only the innermost loop. However, you can use a numeric argument to exit or continue at higher levels of nested loops.

Consider the following example demonstrating nested loops with labeled break and continue statements:

```
#!/bin/bash

for i in {1..3}; do
  for j in {1..3}; do
    if [ $i -eq 2 ] && [ $j -eq 2 ]; then
      echo "Breaking both loops at i=$i, j=$j"
      break 2
    fi
    echo "i=$i, j=$j"
  done
done
```

In this case, the script will break out of both loops when i equals 2 and j equals 2. The output will be:

```
i=1, j=1
i=1, j=2
i=1, j=3
i=2, j=1
Breaking both loops at i=2, j=2
```

Similarly, explicit numerical arguments can be applied with the continue statement to control the loop levels more precisely. Below is an example:

```
#!/bin/bash

for i in {1..3}; do
  for j in {1..3}; do
    if [ $i -eq 2 ] && [ $j -eq 2 ]; then
      echo "Continuing outer loop at i=$i, j=$j"
      continue 2
    fi
    echo "i=$i, j=$j"
  done
done
```

Here, the script continues the outer loop when i equals 2 and j equals

2, skipping any remaining iterations of the inner loop for that specific value of i. The script can be verified through its output:

```
i=1, j=1
i=1, j=2
i=1, j=3
i=2, j=1
Continuing outer loop at i=2, j=2
i=3, j=1
i=3, j=2
i=3, j=3
```

Overall, mastering the use of break and continue statements is critical for efficient loop management in Bash scripting, enabling precise control over loop execution flow while enhancing script clarity and functionality.

5.7 Using Select for Menus

The select statement in Bash is a powerful and straightforward method for creating menus within scripts. This control structure provides an interactive prompt that allows users to select an option from a list by entering a corresponding number. The select construct significantly simplifies the process of creating user-friendly interfaces for script execution.

The basic syntax of the select statement is as follows:

```
select variable_name in list
do
    commands
done
```

Here, variable_name is the variable that will store the value of the selected item from the list. Each selection from the list corresponds to a number, starting from 1. When a user makes a selection, the commands within the do block are executed.

To illustrate the usage of select, consider a basic example that presents a menu for selecting a fruit:

```
#!/bin/bash

PS3="Please enter your choice: "
select fruit in Apple Banana Orange Exit
do
    case $fruit in
        Apple)
            echo "You have selected Apple."
            ;;
        Banana)
```

```
            echo "You have selected Banana."
            ;;
        Orange)
            echo "You have selected Orange."
            ;;
        Exit)
            echo "Exiting..."
            break
            ;;
        *)
            echo "Invalid option. Please try again."
            ;;
    esac
done
```

In the script above, the PS3 variable is used to customize the prompt message. Below is a sample output demonstrating how the select menu operates:

```
1) Apple
2) Banana
3) Orange
4) Exit
Please enter your choice:
```

When the user inputs a number corresponding to a menu option, such as 1 for Apple, the script prints the selected fruit:

```
Please enter your choice: 1
You have selected Apple.
Please enter your choice:
```

The select loop continues to prompt the user until they choose the Exit option, which invokes the break statement to exit the loop.

Handling Invalid Input

It is important to handle cases where the user inputs an invalid option. The above script already includes a default case in the case statement to address invalid inputs by displaying an error message:

```
*)
    echo "Invalid option. Please try again."
    ;;
```

Integrating select with Functions

In practice, integrating the select menu with functions can enhance script modularity. Consider the following enhanced version of the fruit selection menu where each menu option triggers a specific function:

```
#!/bin/bash

function select_apple {
    echo "Function: You have selected Apple."
}
```

```
function select_banana {
    echo "Function: You have selected Banana."
}

function select_orange {
    echo "Function: You have selected Orange."
}

PS3="Please enter your choice: "
select fruit in Apple Banana Orange Exit
do
    case $fruit in
        Apple)
            select_apple
            ;;
        Banana)
            select_banana
            ;;
        Orange)
            select_orange
            ;;
        Exit)
            echo "Exiting..."
            break
            ;;
        *)
            echo "Invalid option. Please try again."
            ;;
    esac
done
```

Here, the selection results in the execution of corresponding functions, thereby organizing the script better and keeping the main loop concise.

Customizing the Menu Display

The select construct can be customized further by modifying the prompt and the list display. For instance:

```
#!/bin/bash

PS3="Choose your fruit (1-4): "

select fruit in Apple Banana Orange "I don't like fruits" Exit
do
    case $REPLY in
        1)
            echo "You have selected Apple."
            ;;
        2)
            echo "You have selected Banana."
            ;;
        3)
            echo "You have selected Orange."
            ;;
        4)
            echo "You have selected: I don't like fruits."
            ;;
        5)
            echo "Exiting..."
```

```
            break
            ;;
        *)
            echo "Invalid option. Please try again."
            ;;
    esac
done
```

In this example, REPLY is used to capture the user's raw input number, allowing for more precise control within the case statement. This setup distinctly manages each menu item by its numeric selection rather than the item name itself.

Practical Application

This method of menu selection can be used in various scenarios ranging from simple personal scripts to complex user interfaces in larger automation workflows. Menus can be tailored to guide users through configuration options, task selections, or data entry points, thereby improving user interaction and script functionality.

Cutting across different complexities, the select command remains a highly practical tool due to its clarity and ease of use, emphasizing its importance in versatile script development.

5.8 Nesting Control Structures

Nesting control structures refers to placing one or more control structures within another. This allows for the creation of complex decision-making processes and iterative operations within your Bash scripts. Understanding how to correctly nest control structures is essential for developing sophisticated scripts that can handle multiple conditions and actions efficiently.

The most common control structures used in nesting include conditional statements (if, elif, else), loops (for, while, until), and the case statement. Combining these elements requires meticulous attention to syntax to avoid logical errors and ensure that the script executes as intended.

```
#!/bin/bash

echo "Enter a number between 1 and 10:"
read number

if [ $number -ge 1 ] && [ $number -le 10 ]; then
    echo "Valid number, starting countdown:"
    for (( i=$number; i>0; i-- ))
    do
```

```
        echo $i
    done
    echo "Countdown complete."
else
    echo "Invalid number. Please enter a value between 1 and 10."
fi
```

In this example, a for loop is nested within an if conditional statement. The if statement first checks if the user input is within the valid range. If the condition is true, the nested for loop executes a countdown from the entered number to zero, otherwise, an error message is displayed.

Nesting Conditionals within Loops

Consider a scenario where you need to check multiple conditions inside a loop. Nesting if, elif, and else statements within a loop allows for this.

```
#!/bin/bash

for i in {1..5}
do
    if [ $i -eq 3 ]; then
        echo "i is equal to 3"
    elif [ $i -eq 5 ]; then
        echo "i is equal to 5"
    else
        echo "i is neither 3 nor 5"
    fi
done
```

This script runs a loop five times, checking the value of i during each iteration. Depending on the value of i, different messages are printed. This demonstrates how nested conditionals can be used to create complex conditional logic inside loops.

Using case Statements within Loops

The case statement is beneficial for evaluating a variable against multiple patterns. Nesting case statements within loops can handle various scenarios efficiently.

```
#!/bin/bash

for color in red green blue yellow
do
    case $color in
        red)
            echo "$color is the color of passion."
            ;;
        green)
            echo "$color is the color of nature."
            ;;
        blue)
            echo "$color is the color of the ocean."
            ;;
        yellow)
```

```
            echo "$color is the color of the sun."
            ;;
        *)
            echo "$color is a unique color."
            ;;
    esac
done
```

This script iterates over a list of colors, using a case statement to print a unique message for each color. The case statement is nested within the for loop, demonstrating how to manage multiple conditions inside a loop structure clearly and concisely.

Combining Multiple Nested Control Structures

Complex scripts often require a combination of different nested control structures. The following example combines loops and conditional statements within another loop.

```
#!/bin/bash

for outer in {1..3}
do
    echo "Outer loop iteration: $outer"
    for inner in {1..3}
    do
        if [ $inner -eq 2 ]; then
            echo " Inner loop, skipping value $inner"
            continue
        fi
        echo " Inner loop iteration: $inner"
    done
done
```

In this script, an outer for loop iterates three times. Within this loop, an inner for loop also iterates three times, but skips the value 2 due to the nested if statement that uses the continue statement. This example demonstrates how to handle more complex logic with nested control structures.

Understanding and effectively using nested control structures enhances your ability to create robust and feature-rich Bash scripts. Mastery of this concept is fundamental for scripting intricate workflows and handling multifaceted conditions and iterations within your programs.

5.9 Writing Complex Conditions

In advanced Bash scripting, writing complex conditions is crucial for making scripts more dynamic and flexible. Complex conditions typically involve a combination of multiple conditional expressions using logical operators such as && (logical AND), || (logical OR), and the ! (negation) operator.

When writing complex conditions, it's essential to understand the precedence of these logical operators to ensure expressions evaluate as intended. The ! operator has the highest precedence, followed by &&, and then ||. Parentheses can be used to group expressions and override the default precedence.

Below are several examples demonstrating how to construct complex conditions in Bash scripting:

```
#!/bin/bash

# Assigning values to variables
value1=10
value2=20
value3=30

# Using logical AND (&&) and OR (||) in a single if statement
if [[ $value1 -lt $value2 && $value2 -lt $value3 ]]; then
    echo "Both conditions are true."
fi

# Using logical OR (||) with negation (!)
if [[ $value1 -gt $value3 || ! ($value2 -eq 20) ]]; then
    echo "One of the conditions is true or value2 is not 20."
fi
```

In the above examples, the first if statement checks if both $value1 is less than $value2 and $value2 is less than $value3. If both conditions are met, the statement inside the if block executes. In the second if statement, it checks if either $value1 is greater than $value3 or $value2 is not equal to 20. If either condition is true, the statement inside the if block executes.

Combining Multiple Conditional Expressions

Combining multiple conditional expressions often makes the script more readable and maintainable. Using nested conditions and logical operators can simplify complex decision-making.

Consider the following script that determines the type and range of a number:

```
#!/bin/bash

# Read a number from user input
read -p "Enter a number: " num

# Determine the range and type of the number
if (( num > 0 )); then
    if (( num < 10 )); then
        echo "The number is positive and single-digit."
    elif (( num < 100 )); then
        echo "The number is positive and two-digit."
    else
        echo "The number is positive and has three or more digits."
    fi
else
    echo "The number is zero or negative."
fi
```

This script uses nested if statements to handle different ranges of positive numbers. If the input num is greater than 0, the script further checks if the number falls into single, two, or more digit categories, providing appropriate feedback.

Using Complex Conditions with Case Statements

Case statements are another control structure in Bash scripting that can benefit from complex conditions. For example, matching multiple patterns within a case block can be achieved by using logical OR (|) inside each pattern.

```
#!/bin/bash

# Read the day of the week from user input
read -p "Enter a day of the week: " day

# Convert the day to lowercase
day=$(echo $day | tr '[:upper:]' '[:lower:]')

# Determine the type of the day
case $day in
    monday|tuesday|wednesday|thursday|friday)
        echo "$day is a weekday."
        ;;
    saturday|sunday)
        echo "$day is a weekend."
        ;;
    *)
        echo "Invalid input."
        ;;
esac
```

In this example, the case statement checks if the user input matches any of the specified weekday or weekend patterns. If the input matches one of the specified patterns, the corresponding message is displayed. This approach simplifies the logic while maintaining readability and structure.

Handling Exit Status in Complex Conditions

Bash scripting heavily relies on exit statuses to determine the success or failure of commands and scripts. Integrating complex conditions with exit statuses allows for robust error handling and flow control.

Consider a script that checks the availability of multiple services:

```
#!/bin/bash

# Check if services are running
service1_status=$(systemctl is-active apache2)
service2_status=$(systemctl is-active mysql)

if [[ $service1_status == "active" && $service2_status == "active" ]]; then
    echo "Both Apache2 and MySQL services are running."
    exit 0
else
    if [[ $service1_status != "active" ]]; then
        echo "Apache2 service is not running."
    fi
    if [[ $service2_status != "active" ]]; then
        echo "MySQL service is not running."
    fi
    exit 1
fi
```

This script checks the status of the Apache2 and MySQL services. If both services are running, it prints a success message and exits with status 0. If either service is not running, it prints an error message for each inactive service and exits with status 1.

Evaluating String Conditions

While numeric conditions are common in Bash scripting, string evaluations are equally important. Complex string conditions can be handled effectively using string comparison operators and logical operators.

```
#!/bin/bash

# Read two strings from user input
read -p "Enter the first string: " str1
read -p "Enter the second string: " str2

# Check for different string conditions
if [[ -z $str1 || -z $str2 ]]; then
```

```
    echo "One or both strings are empty."
elif [[ $str1 == $str2 ]]; then
    echo "The strings are identical."
else
    echo "The strings are different."
fi
```

This script evaluates different conditions involving two input strings. It checks for empty strings using the -z operator, compares the strings for equality using the == operator, and handles cases where the strings are different.

Combining various types of evaluations and logical operators offers a versatile approach to writing complex conditions in Bash scripting, ensuring scripts are robust, efficient, and capable of handling a wide range of scenarios.

5.10 Handling Errors and Exit Status

Error handling is an essential aspect of writing robust Bash scripts. To effectively manage and respond to errors within your scripts, it is crucial to understand the concept of exit status. In Bash, each command returns an exit status, a numerical value that signifies whether the command was executed successfully or encountered an issue.

Commands typically follow the convention:

- An exit status of 0 indicates that the command executed successfully without any errors.
- A non-zero exit status indicates that the command encountered an error.

To retrieve and act upon the exit status of the last executed command, you use the special variable $?. Let us examine an example that demonstrates the usage of the $? variable:

```
#!/bin/bash
echo "Running the command: ls /nonexistent_directory"
ls /nonexistent_directory
status=$?
if [ $status -eq 0 ]; then
    echo "Command executed successfully."
else
    echo "Command failed with exit status $status."
fi
```

In this script, the ls command attempts to list a non-existent directory. The exit status of the ls command is captured in the variable status. The if statement then checks the value of status to determine if the command succeeded or failed.

It is also common to make use of the set -e option to ensure that the script exits immediately if any command exits with a non-zero status. The set -e command is particularly useful in scripts where error conditions should prevent subsequent command execution. Below is an illustration of using set -e in a script:

```
#!/bin/bash
set -e
echo "Creating directory test_dir"
mkdir test_dir

echo "Creating file test_file inside test_dir"
touch test_dir/test_file

echo "Trying to change directory to non\_existent\_dir"
cd non\_existent\_dir

echo "This line will not be executed because the previous command failed."
```

In this example, the script will terminate immediately after the cd non_-existent_dir command fails, without executing any of the subsequent commands.

However, there are scenarios where you might want more granular control over error handling, rather than exiting immediately. In such situations, you can leverage the trap command to capture errors and perform cleanup tasks or error logging. Here is an example of using trap for error handling:

```
#!/bin/bash

trap 'catchError' ERR

function catchError {
    echo "An error occurred. Performing cleanup."
    # Add cleanup commands here
    exit 1
}

echo "Running command that will succeed"
ls /

echo "Running command that will fail"
ls /nonexistent_directory

echo "This line will not be executed because the script exits in catchError."
```

In this script, the trap command is used to bind the catchError function to the ERR signal, which is triggered whenever a command fails. The catchError function will execute whenever an error occurs, allowing for custom error handling and cleanup processes.

Another important aspect of error handling is creating scripts that can gracefully handle and log errors to assist with debugging and maintaining code. Here's an enhanced script example that includes more comprehensive error handling:

```
#!/bin/bash

# Function to log messages
logMessage() {
    local MSG="$1"
    echo "$(date +'%Y-%m-%d %H:%M:%S') - $MSG"
}

# Function to handle errors
handleError() {
    local LAST_COMMAND="$1"
    local EXIT_STATUS="$2"
    logMessage "ERROR: Command '$LAST_COMMAND' exited with status
        $EXIT_STATUS."
    exit $EXIT_STATUS
}

# Trap ERR to call handleError function
trap 'handleError "$BASH_COMMAND" $?' ERR

# Sample commands
logMessage "Running command: mkdir test_error_handling"
mkdir test_error_handling

logMessage "Running command: touch test_error_handling/file"
touch test_error_handling/file

logMessage "Running command: ls /nonexistent_directory"
ls /nonexistent_directory

logMessage "This line will not be executed if previous command fails."
```

This script includes a logMessage function to standardize log formatting and a handleError function to display detailed error messages, which helps to identify the command that caused the failure. The trap command is set to call handleError whenever an error occurs, providing both error handling and logging functionality.

Effectively managing exit statuses and handling errors is critical for writing reliable and maintainable Bash scripts. Understanding how to leverage the $? variable, set -e, and the trap command enables you to create scripts that can handle errors gracefully, enhance debugging capabilities, and ensure robust execution of commands.

Chapter 6

Functions in Bash

This chapter covers the use of functions in Bash scripting, including defining and calling functions, handling function arguments and return values, and the distinction between local and global variables. Readers will learn to use functions effectively within scripts, debug them, and write reusable functions. The chapter also discusses organizing functions in files, parameter expansion in functions, and best practices for function usage.

6.1 Introduction to Functions

In Bash scripting, functions are a fundamental construct that allows for modular programming. They encapsulate a block of code that performs a specific task, which can be called multiple times within a script. Functions provide several advantages such as improved code readability, reuse, and easier maintenance.

To define a function in Bash, the following syntax is used:

```
function_name() {
    # commands
}
```

Alternatively, functions can also be defined without the function keyword:

```
function_name {
    # commands
}
```

The choice between these two styles is largely a matter of personal or team preference, as both accomplish the same result.

Once a function is defined, it can be called simply by its name:

```
function_name
```

This simplicity makes functions a versatile tool in scripting.

Example of Function Definition and Invocation:

```
greet() {
    echo "Hello, $1!"
}

greet "Alice"
```

```
Hello, Alice!
```

In this example, the function greet takes a single argument and prints a greeting message. When the function is called with the argument "Alice", the output is "Hello, Alice!".

Understanding and correctly utilizing functions involves knowing how to handle arguments and return values. Functions can accept any number of arguments. Inside the function, these arguments are accessible using positional parameters $1, $2, and so on, analogous to how a script accesses its arguments.

Example of Function with Multiple Arguments:

```
add_numbers() {
    local sum=$(( $1 + $2 ))
    echo $sum
}

result=$(add_numbers 5 10)
echo "Sum: $result"
```

```
Sum: 15
```

Here, the function add_numbers takes two arguments, computes their sum, and returns the result. The local keyword is used to define a local variable, which will be discussed in detail in the section on local and global variables.

Functions in Bash can also return values. However, unlike some other programming languages, Bash functions do not return values via a return statement for data but rather use the echo command to output the value, which can then be captured by command substitution.

Returning Values from Functions:

```
uppercase() {
    local input="$1"
    echo "${input^^}"
}

result=$(uppercase "hello")
echo "Uppercase: $result"
```

```
Uppercase: HELLO
```

In the uppercase function, the parameter $1 is converted to uppercase using parameter expansion ${input^} and then returned. The calling code captures this output using command substitution $(...).

Concepts of scope are crucial in working with functions. Variables in Bash can be either global or local. Global variables are accessible throughout the script, whereas local variables are confined to the function in which they are declared. Using the local keyword when declaring variables prevents unintended interactions with variables outside the function.

To illustrate, consider the following example:

```
global_var="I am global"

print_vars() {
    local local_var="I am local"
    echo "$global_var"
    echo "$local_var"
}

print_vars

echo "$global_var"
# Uncommenting the next line causes an error
# echo "$local_var"
```

```
I am global
I am local
I am global
```

Here, local_var is only accessible within the print_vars function, while global_var is accessible both inside and outside of the function.

Functions are also instrumental in dividing a script into logical segments. This facilitates debugging, as smaller code segments are easier to test and verify. By organizing code into functions, complex scripts become manageable, allowing for incremental development and troubleshooting.

In addition to encapsulating reusable logic, functions can leverage recursion, where a function calls itself. This must be handled with care to avoid infinite loops, as shown below:

```
factorial() {
    if [ "$1" -le 1 ]; then
        echo 1
    else
        local temp=$(( $1 - 1 ))
        local result=$(factorial $temp)
        echo $(( $1 * result ))
    fi
}

result=$(factorial 5)
echo "Factorial of 5 is: $result"
```

```
Factorial of 5 is: 120
```

This recursive factorial function calculates the factorial of a number. The base case returns 1 when the input is less than or equal to 1. For other cases, the function calls itself with decremented values until reaching the base case.

Applying these concepts, developers can build robust and scalable Bash scripts. The subsequent sections will delve deeper into advanced topics, such as handling function arguments in detail, return values, and best practices for writing and organizing functions. By mastering these, one can achieve expert proficiency in Bash scripting, enabling efficient and effective script development.

6.2 Defining and Calling Functions

Defining functions in Bash scripting is a crucial aspect of writing modular and maintainable code. Functions allow you to encapsulate a sequence of commands that can be easily reused throughout your script. A function in Bash is essentially a block of code that can be called with a name, possibly taking parameters and producing output or performing side effects.

To define a function in Bash, you use the function keyword or the alternative syntax without it. Both methods are widely accepted, though the function keyword is more explicit in its purpose. Here is the general syntax for defining a function:

```
function_name() {
```

```
    # commands
}
```

Alternatively, you can also define a function like this:

```
function function_name {
    # commands
}
```

An example function that prints "Hello, World!" is as follows:

```
greet() {
    echo "Hello, World!"
}
```

To call or invoke the greet function, simply use its name:

```
greet
```

When executed, the script will display:

```
Hello, World!
```

Function names follow the same naming rules as variable names. They should start with a letter or an underscore and can contain alphanumeric characters and underscores.

Handling Positional Parameters in Functions

Functions can take positional parameters, which are accessed in the same way as script-level positional parameters. Inside the function, $1, $2, and so on represent the arguments passed to the function.

```
add_numbers() {
    local number1=$1
    local number2=$2
    echo $((number1 + number2))
}
```

Calling this add_numbers function with two arguments:

```
add_numbers 3 5
```

The output will be:

```
8
```

Returning Values from Functions

In Bash, a function can return a status code to the calling context, similar to how a script returns a status code upon completion. This is done using the `return` command followed by a numeric value between 0 and 255. By convention, a return value of 0 indicates success, while any non-zero value indicates failure.

```
check_number() {
    local number=$1
    if [ $number -gt 10 ]; then
        return 0
    else
        return 1
    fi
}
```

You can capture the return value of the function using the special variable `$?` immediately after the function call.

```
check_number 15
if [ $? -eq 0 ]; then
    echo "Number is greater than 10."
else
    echo "Number is less than or equal to 10."
fi
```

The output will be:

```
Number is greater than 10.
```

Alternatively, you can use command substitution to capture the output of a function:

```
square() {
    local value=$1
    echo $((value * value))
}

result=$(square 4)
echo "The square of 4 is $result"
```

The output will be:

```
The square of 4 is 16
```

Using Global and Local Variables

By default, variables defined within a function are global, meaning their values are accessible and modifiable outside the function scope. This can lead to unintended side effects; hence it is good practice to use local variables within functions. The local keyword declares a variable's scope to be local to the function, protecting it from being altered outside.

```
increment() {
    local counter=$1
    counter=$((counter + 1))
    echo $counter
}

counter=10
result=$(increment $counter)
echo "Counter is $counter"
echo "Result is $result"
```

The output will be:

```
Counter is 10
Result is 11
```

This ensures that the counter variable outside the function remains unchanged.

Functions in Bash enable the construction of well-structured and reusable code. By defining and calling functions thoughtfully, handling positional parameters, managing return values, and using local variables, scripts become more modular, maintainable, and less error-prone.

6.3 Function Arguments and Return Values

In Bash, functions provide an efficient way to manage and reuse code. They can accept arguments and return values, which makes them powerful tools for performing complex tasks. Understanding how to work with function arguments and return values effectively is essential for proficient Bash scripting.

Functions in Bash can receive arguments similarly to scripts. When a function is called, any arguments provided to it are accessible within the function via positional parameters $1, $2, ..., $n, where n is the number of arguments supplied.

```
# Function definition
greet() {
    echo "Hello, $1!"
}

# Calling the function with an argument
greet "Alice"
```

The output of the above script is:

```
Hello, Alice!
```

In the greet function, $1 refers to the first argument passed to the function, which in this case is "Alice". For functions requiring multiple arguments, $2, $3, etc., can be used.

Managing a large number of arguments can be facilitated by using special parameters like $@ and $#, which represent all arguments passed to the function:

```
process_arguments() {
    echo "All arguments: $@"
    echo "Total number of arguments: $#"
}
process_arguments "arg1" "arg2" "arg3"
```

The output of the above script is:

```
All arguments: arg1 arg2 arg3
Total number of arguments: 3
```

$@ provides a space-separated list of all arguments, while $# gives the number of arguments.

Another critical aspect of function utilization in Bash is the return value. Unlike other programming languages, Bash functions do not have a return statement that returns a value directly. Instead, they use the exit status of the last command executed within the function. The exit status can be retrieved using the return command followed by an integer value, where 0 typically signifies success and any non-zero value indicates an error or differing condition.

```
check_file() {
    if [ -f "$1" ]; then
        echo "File exists."
        return 0
    else
        echo "File does not exist."
        return 1
    fi
}

check_file "testfile.txt"
echo "Function exit status: $?"
```

The output of the above script depends on the existence of testfile.txt:

```
File does not exist.
Function exit status: 1
```

To capture and utilize the exit status or returned value of a function,

$? is used immediately after the function call. This exit status can be stored in a variable if needed for further processing:

```
check_file "testfile.txt"
status=$?
if [ $status -eq 0 ]; then
   echo "The file check passed."
else
   echo "The file check failed."
fi
```

Additional flexibility can be achieved by using global variables when a more complex return value is necessary. Care must be taken to avoid such variables clashing with ones outside the scope of the function. By convention, global variables are usually declared at the beginning of the script and are given explicit names often written in uppercase for readability.

```
# Global variable declaration
RESULT=""

check_file() {
   if [ -f "$1" ]; then
      RESULT="File exists"
   else
      RESULT="File does not exist"
   fi
}

check_file "testfile.txt"
echo "Function result: $RESULT"
```

In this example, the function check_file alters the global variable RESULT, providing a meaningful textual result that can be used outside the function's scope.

Moreover, to signal more detailed information back to the calling script, Bash functions can output their result directly. This output can then be captured using command substitution.

```
sum() {
   echo $(($1 + $2))
}

result=$(sum 3 4)
echo "Sum is: $result"
```

In this example, the function sum prints the result of adding two numbers. The caller captures this output via command substitution $(...) and stores it in the variable result.

Effective argument handling and return value management are fundamental to constructing robust and modular scripts. By leveraging these tools, the reusability and maintainability of Bash scripts are significantly enhanced.

6.4 Local vs. Global Variables in Functions

In Bash scripting, understanding the scope of variables—whether they are local or global—is crucial for writing maintainable and bug-free scripts. A variable's scope determines its accessibility within parts of the script. This section delves into the distinctions between local and global variables, illustrates how to declare and use them within functions, and provides examples to elucidate these concepts.

Global variables are those that can be accessed and modified from anywhere within the script after their declaration. They are defined outside of any function. Below is an example illustrating the use of a global variable.

```
#!/bin/bash

# Declare a global variable
global_var="I am a global variable"

# Function to print the global variable
print_global() {
    echo $global_var
}

# Call the function
print_global
```

```
Output:
I am a global variable
```

In the script above, global_var is a global variable defined outside the print_global function. When the function is called, it can access and print the value of global_var without any issues.

Conversely, local variables are those whose scope is limited to the function in which they are declared. These variables are created using the local keyword. Once the function terminates, the local variable is destroyed, and its value is no longer accessible. Below is an example demonstrating the use of a local variable.

```
#!/bin/bash

# Function with a local variable
print_local() {
    local local_var="I am a local variable"
    echo $local_var
}
```

```
# Call the function
print_local

# Try to access the local variable outside the function
echo $local_var
```

```
Output:
I am a local variable
(empty line)
```

In this script, local_var is declared inside the print_local function using the local keyword. Attempting to access local_var outside the function results in an empty output because local_var is not accessible beyond the function's scope.

To further illustrate the difference, consider the following script where both global and local variables interact within a function.

```
#!/bin/bash

# Declare a global variable
var="global"

modify_vars() {
    # Declare a local variable with the same name
    local var="local"
    echo "Inside function: $var"
}

# Call the function
modify_vars

# Print the global variable
echo "Outside function: $var"
```

```
Output:
Inside function: local
Outside function: global
```

Here, var is initially a global variable. Inside the function modify_vars, a local variable named var is declared. The function modifies and prints its local var, while outside the function, the global var remains unchanged. This illustrates the concept of variable shadowing, where a local variable with the same name temporarily hides the global variable within the function's scope.

When dealing with more complex scripts where functions call other functions, it's essential to keep track of variable scopes to avoid unintended side effects. Consider an example where multiple functions interact:

```
#!/bin/bash

# Declare a global variable
global_message="Hello from the global scope"
```

```
first_function() {
    # Declare a local variable
    local local_message="Hello from the first function"
    echo $local_message

    # Call a nested function
    second_function
}

second_function() {
    echo $global_message
    echo $local_message
}

# Call the first function
first_function
```

```
Output:
Hello from the first function
Hello from the global scope
(empty line)
```

In this script, first_function declares a local variable local_message, prints it, and then calls second_function. The second_function has access to the global variable global_message, but it cannot access the local variable local_message from first_function, leading to an empty output for the second echo statement within second_function.

By judiciously using local variables within functions, scripts become more modular and less prone to errors caused by unintentional modifications to global variables. This practice enhances code readability and maintainability, especially in large scripts. Understanding and managing variable scope is fundamental for effective function design and script organization in Bash.

6.5 Using Functions in Scripts

Incorporating functions into your Bash scripts is a crucial step for making your code more modular, readable, and easier to maintain. By encapsulating repetitive tasks within functions, you can significantly reduce code redundancy and enhance the overall clarity of your scripts.

To begin with, let's revisit the fundamental structure of a Bash function:

```
function_name() {
    commands
}
```

You can call this function by simply using its name:

```
function_name
```

To illustrate how functions can be effectively used in Bash scripts, consider a script that processes log files. Assume we want to perform multiple operations on the log files, such as counting lines, extracting specific entries, and archiving old logs. Each of these tasks can be elegantly handled by separate functions.

```
#!/bin/bash

# Function to count the number of lines in a log file
count_lines() {
    local file=$1
    wc -l < "$file"
}

# Function to extract error entries from a log file
extract_errors() {
    local file=$1
    grep "ERROR" "$file"
}

# Function to archive old log files
archive_logs() {
    local file=$1
    gzip "$file"
}

# Main script logic
log_file="system.log"

# Count and display the number of lines
line_count=$(count_lines "$log_file")
echo "Number of lines: $line_count"

# Extract and display error entries
echo "Error entries:"
extract_errors "$log_file"

# Archive the log file
archive_logs "$log_file"
echo "Log file archived."
```

In this script:

- The count_lines function calculates the number of lines in a specified file using the wc -l command.
- The extract_errors function filters and prints the error entries from the log file using the grep command to search for the string "ERROR".
- The archive_logs function compresses the log file using the gzip command.

These discrete functions enhance script organization by isolating specific tasks. This modular approach offers several advantages:

- Reducing redundancy: Functions can be reused multiple times within the script without having to rewrite the same code.
- Enhancing readability: Functions with descriptive names make the script's logic clearer.
- Simplifying debugging: Functions can be tested separately, facilitating easier identification and correction of errors.

Moreover, functions can be defined to accept parameters, which adds flexibility. For example, the functions count_lines, extract_errors, and archive_logs were all designed to accept a file name as an argument. This allows them to operate on any given file, rather than being hard-coded to a specific one.

An important aspect of using functions in scripts is understanding the scope of variables. Variables declared within a function are local to that function unless explicitly marked as global. This helps to prevent conflicts between variables used in different parts of the script. Consider the following example:

```
#!/bin/bash

# Global variable
result_file="results.txt"

# Function to perform a calculation and store the result
calculate() {
    local x=$1
    local y=$2
    local result=$((x + y))
    echo "Result: $result"
    echo $result >> "$result_file"
}

# Main script logic
calculate 3 5
calculate 10 20

echo "Calculation results stored in $result_file"
```

In this script:

- The variable result in the calculate function is declared with the local keyword to ensure it is confined to the function's scope.
- The global variable result_file is accessed within the function to

append results, demonstrating how local and global variables can interact.

Adopting this approach helps to avoid unexpected behaviors caused by unintentional modifications to variables outside their intended scope.

Let's also consider an example involving conditional logic and loops within functions, providing a more complex use case:

```
#!/bin/bash

# Function to evaluate disk usage and warn if above a threshold
check_disk_usage() {
    local threshold=$1
    local usage=$(df / | tail -1 | awk '{print $5}' | tr -d '%')

    if (( usage > threshold )); then
        echo "Warning: Disk usage is above the threshold of $threshold%. Current usage:
              $usage%."
    else
        echo "Disk usage is within safe limits. Current usage: $usage%."
    fi
}

# Function to monitor system load over a period of time
monitor_system_load() {
    local duration=$1
    local interval=$2
    echo "Monitoring system load for $duration seconds at $interval-second intervals."

    for ((i = 0; i < duration; i += interval)); do
        uptime
        sleep "$interval"
    done
}

# Main script logic
echo "Starting system checks"

disk_usage_threshold=80
check_disk_usage "$disk_usage_threshold"

monitor_duration=60
monitor_interval=10
monitor_system_load "$monitor_duration" "$monitor_interval"

echo "System checks completed."
```

In this script:

- The check_disk_usage function checks the disk usage against a specified threshold, utilizing conditionals to provide appropriate warnings.
- The monitor_system_load function monitors system load at regular intervals, exemplifying the use of loops within functions.

Through these illustrative examples and detailed explanations, it is evident that using functions in Bash scripts greatly enhances the modularity, readability, and maintainability of the script code. These principles are central to effective Bash scripting and are applicable across diverse scripting scenarios.

6.6 Debugging Functions

Debugging functions in Bash scripting is a critical skill for ensuring the reliability and correctness of scripts. Identifying and resolving issues within functions can help maintain the smooth operation of larger script workflows. In this section, we will cover various techniques and tools available for debugging Bash functions.

To troubleshoot functions, it's essential to have a methodology that allows you to pinpoint errors efficiently. The following strategies can be leveraged for effective debugging:

1. Using set command with debug options:

The set command in Bash can be used with various options to aid in debugging. Key options include:

- -x: Enables a mode of the shell where all executed commands are printed to the terminal.
- -v: Prints shell input lines as they are read.
- -u: Treats unset variables as an error and exits immediately.
- -e: Exits immediately if a command exits with a non-zero status. This is particularly useful for scripts where you want to stop execution on any error.

To enable these options within your debugging session, use the following syntax within the script:

```
#!/bin/bash
set -x
# Your script here
set +x
```

Here is an example of debugging a function with the set -x option:

```
#!/bin/bash
```

```
my_function() {
    set -x
    local result=$(( $1 + $2 ))
    echo "The result is $result"
    set +x
}

my_function 2 3
```

When you run this script, you will see each command and its results printed to the terminal, providing a step-by-step trace of the function execution.

2. Employing echo **statements:**

Inserting echo statements at various points within a function can help you verify the flow of execution and the state of variables at specific stages. This method, though traditional, is still widely used due to its simplicity and effectiveness.

Consider the following example, where echo is used for debugging:

```
#!/bin/bash

calculate_sum() {
    echo "Entering calculate_sum function"
    local sum=$(( $1 + $2 ))
    echo "The value of the first parameter: $1"
    echo "The value of the second parameter: $2"
    echo "Sum is $sum"
    echo "Exiting calculate_sum function"
}

calculate_sum 5 7
```

The output will provide a clear trace of variable values and the execution flow, making it easier to identify any discrepancies.

```
Entering calculate_sum function
The value of the first parameter: 5
The value of the second parameter: 7
Sum is 12
Exiting calculate_sum function
```

3. Using trap **command:**

The trap command can catch signals and execute specified commands when a signal is received. This is particularly useful for handling errors and debugging.

Example of using trap to catch errors:

```
#!/bin/bash

trap 'echo "Error occurred at line $LINENO"; exit' ERR
```

```
divide_numbers() {
    local num1=$1
    local num2=$2
    echo "Dividing $num1 by $num2"
    local result=$(( num1 / num2 ))
    echo "Result: $result"
}

divide_numbers 10 0
```

When a division by zero error occurs, the trap command will capture it and display the line number where the error occurred.

```
Dividing 10 by 0
Error occurred at line 10
```

4. Utilizing DEBUG and PS4 variables:

Bash provides special debugging hooks via the DEBUG and PS4 variables. The DEBUG trap allows executing a command before every simple command, while PS4 can format the debugging output.

Example of using DEBUG trap and PS4:

```
#!/bin/bash

PS4='+ ${BASH_SOURCE}:${LINENO}:${FUNCNAME[0]}() '
trap 'echo "Executing command: $BASH_COMMAND"' DEBUG

multiply_numbers() {
    local num1=$1
    local num2=$2
    local result=$(( num1 * num2 ))
    echo "Multiplication result: $result"
}

multiply_numbers 4 5
```

The output will provide detailed information about script execution, including the file name, line number, and function name.

```
Executing command: local num1=$1
+ script.sh:8:multiply_numbers() num1=$1
Executing command: local num2=$2
+ script.sh:9:multiply_numbers() num2=$2
Executing command: local result=$(( num1 * num2 ))
+ script.sh:10:multiply_numbers() result=$(( num1 * num2 ))
Executing command: echo "Multiplication result: $result"
+ script.sh:11:multiply_numbers() echo "Multiplication result: 20"
Multiplication result: 20
```

Combining these techniques will help create a robust debugging toolkit, facilitating the development of error-free, efficient bash functions.

6.7 Writing Reusable Functions

When writing scripts, the goal should always be to develop modular, reusable code that can be applied in various contexts. This approach not only enhances code readability but also makes debugging and maintenance significantly easier. Reusable functions are essential components of this paradigm. In this section, we will delve into the best practices and methodologies for constructing reusable functions in Bash scripting.

A reusable function should be generic enough to handle a wide range of inputs and scenarios while maintaining the core functionality. Let's walk through the steps involved in creating such functions, accompanied by detailed examples and techniques.

To start, let's define a simple function designed to perform basic arithmetic operations. The function will accept three arguments: two numbers and the operation type.

```
#!/bin/bash

# Function to perform basic arithmetic operations
basic_arithmetic() {
  local num1="$1"
  local num2="$2"
  local operation="$3"

  case "$operation" in
    add)
      echo "$((num1 + num2))"
      ;;
    subtract)
      echo "$((num1 - num2))"
      ;;
    multiply)
      echo "$((num1 * num2))"
      ;;
    divide)
      if [ "$num2" -ne 0 ]; then
        echo "$((num1 / num2))"
      else
        echo "Division by zero error"
        return 1
      fi
      ;;
    *)
      echo "Invalid operation"
      return 2
      ;;
  esac
}

# Example calls to the function
result=$(basic_arithmetic 10 5 add)
echo "10 + 5 = $result"
```

```
result=$(basic_arithmetic 10 0 divide)
echo "10 / 0 = $result"
```

In this example, we have created a function named basic_arithmetic that handles addition, subtraction, multiplication, and division. The case statement inside the function uses the third argument to determine which operation to perform. By using local variables within the function, we ensure that num1, num2, and operation do not interfere with or get overwritten by variables outside the function.

Parameter Validation

To make the function more robust, it is important to include parameter validation. This ensures that the function behaves predictably even when it receives unexpected input. Let's enhance the previous function to include parameter checks.

```
#!/bin/bash

# Function to perform basic arithmetic operations with parameter validation
enhanced_arithmetic() {
  local num1="$1"
  local num2="$2"
  local operation="$3"

  # Check if proper number of arguments is passed
  if [ "$#" -ne 3 ]; then
    echo "Usage: enhanced_arithmetic <num1> <num2> <operation>"
    return 1
  fi

  # Check if num1 and num2 are integers
  if ! [[ "$num1" =~ ^-?[0-9]+$ ]] || ! [[ "$num2" =~ ^-?[0-9]+$ ]]; then
    echo "Both num1 and num2 should be integers."
    return 1
  fi

  case "$operation" in
    add)
      echo "$((num1 + num2))"
      ;;
    subtract)
      echo "$((num1 - num2))"
      ;;
    multiply)
      echo "$((num1 * num2))"
      ;;
    divide)
      if [ "$num2" -ne 0 ]; then
        echo "$((num1 / num2))"
      else
        echo "Division by zero error"
        return 1
      fi
      ;;
    *)
```

```
        echo "Invalid operation"
        return 2
        ;;
    esac
}

# Example calls to the function
result=$(enhanced_arithmetic 10 5 add)
echo "10 + 5 = $result"

result=$(enhanced_arithmetic 10 0 divide)
echo "10 / 0 = $result"
```

Documentation and Commenting

Writing reusable functions also involves clear and concise documentation. This helps other developers, and even your future self, to understand the purpose and usage of the function. Comments should explain the parameters, the function's behavior, and any edge cases it handles.

Adding Help and Usage Information

A well-written reusable function should provide usage information to guide its users. This practice is especially useful for functions intended to be part of larger scripts or libraries. Adding a help option makes the function more intuitive and easier to use.

```
#!/bin/bash

# Function to perform basic arithmetic operations with help option
arithmetic_with_help() {
  local num1="$1"
  local num2="$2"
  local operation="$3"

  if [ "$#" -eq 1 ] && [ "$1" == "--help" ]; then
    echo "Usage: arithmetic_with_help <num1> <num2> <operation>"
    echo "Operations: add, subtract, multiply, divide"
    return 0
  fi

  # Parameter validation
  if [ "$#" -ne 3 ]; then
    echo "Usage: arithmetic_with_help <num1> <num2> <operation>"
    return 1
  fi

  # Check if num1 and num2 are integers
  if ! [[ "$num1" =~ ^-?[0-9]+$ ]] || ! [[ "$num2" =~ ^-?[0-9]+$ ]]; then
    echo "Both num1 and num2 should be integers."
    return 1
  fi

  case "$operation" in
    add)
      echo "$((num1 + num2))"
      ;;
```

```
    subtract)
      echo "$((num1 - num2))"
      ;;
    multiply)
      echo "$((num1 * num2))"
      ;;
    divide)
      if [ "$num2" -ne 0 ]; then
        echo "$((num1 / num2))"
      else
        echo "Division by zero error"
        return 1
      fi
      ;;
    *)
      echo "Invalid operation"
      return 2
      ;;
  esac
}

# Showing help information
arithmetic_with_help --help
```

Testing and Debugging

Testing your functions thoroughly is essential to ensure they perform as expected in different scenarios. Consider edge cases and invalid inputs, and observe how your function behaves. Utilize test scripts and automated testing frameworks like BATS (Bash Automated Testing System) to validate functionality systematically.

```
#!/usr/bin/env bats

@test "addition" {
  run ./your_script.sh 5 3 add
  [ "$status" -eq 0 ]
  [ "$output" -eq 8 ]
}

@test "division by zero" {
  run ./your_script.sh 5 0 divide
  [ "$status" -eq 1 ]
  [ "$output" == "Division by zero error" ]
}
```

Following these practices will improve the reliability and reusability of your Bash functions, enabling them to be integrated seamlessly into larger projects and scripts. By focusing on modular design, parameter validation, documentation, and thorough testing, you become proficient at writing robust, reusable components in Bash scripting.

6.8 Organizing Functions in Files

Effective management of Bash functions often involves organizing them into separate files. This practice not only enhances readability but also facilitates reuse and maintenance. In this section, the methods used to organize functions within separate files and the techniques to call these functions from other scripts will be explored comprehensively.

To begin with, consider separating your functions into a file named functions.sh. This file could contain multiple function definitions which can be collectively utilized by a main script or other scripts. Here's an example of how the functions.sh file might look like:

```
# functions.sh

greet() {
    local name=$1
    echo "Hello, $name"
}

sum() {
    local num1=$1
    local num2=$2
    echo $(($num1 + $num2))
}
```

The file functions.sh now contains two function definitions: greet() and sum(). These functions are not immediately executable in isolation; they need to be sourced or included in other scripts where their functionality is required.

To use these functions in another script, you can source the functions.sh file. This operation makes all the functions defined in functions.sh available in the current script. For instance, the main script main.sh can include these functions as follows:

```
# main.sh

source ./functions.sh

greet "Alice"
result=$(sum 5 10)
echo "The sum is $result"
```

Running main.sh will output:

```
Hello, Alice
The sum is 15
```

It is crucial to ensure that the path to functions.sh in the source command is correct relative to the location of the main script. The source command, also known by its alias ., reads and executes the content of the file provided, effectively making its functions and variables available for use.

For larger and more complex projects, organizing functions into logically grouped files enhances maintainability. For example, you could have different files for database operations, string manipulations, and system utilities:

```
# db_functions.sh

query_db() {
    local query=$1
    # Placeholder for database query implementation
    echo "Executing: $query"
}

# string_functions.sh

to_upper() {
    local input_string=$1
    echo "${input_string^^}"
}

# system_functions.sh

check_disk_usage() {
    df -h
}
```

The main script can now source multiple files as needed:

```
# main.sh

source ./db_functions.sh
source ./string_functions.sh
source ./system_functions.sh

query_db "SELECT * FROM users"
uppercase_string=$(to_upper "hello")
echo "Uppercase: $uppercase_string"
check_disk_usage
```

Running the updated main.sh leads to:

```
Executing: SELECT * FROM users
Uppercase: HELLO
Filesystem      Size  Used Avail Use% Mounted on
/dev/sda1        50G   30G   18G  63% /
...
```

Organizing functions into separate files also facilitates version control. With each function file managed individually, updates and bug fixes can be tracked distinctly. This separation aids in collaborative projects where different team members may work on designated files without causing conflicts.

Furthermore, it aids in implementing modular designs. Each function file can be seen as a module providing specific functionalities, thereby enabling a more structured and modular scripting architecture. This modular approach encourages code reuse, reducing redundancy and potential errors.

Here are some best practices when organizing functions into files:

- **Group functions logically:** Functions that perform related tasks should reside in the same file. This logical grouping simplifies locating and updating functions.
- **Use descriptive filenames:** The filename should reflect the functionalities of the functions contained within. For instance, network_functions.sh for network-related functions.
- **Write clear comments:** Including comments that describe what each function does, its arguments, and its expected output aids future maintenance.
- **Avoid redundant sourcing:** Source function files only once per script to avoid potential issues with repeated definitions. Guard conditions can be implemented if necessary.

Implementing a modular function organization strategy in your Bash scripts leads to more readable, maintainable, and reusable code. This approach supports orderly script management, particularly beneficial when working within large and complex systems.

6.9 Parameter Expansion in Functions

Parameter expansion is a crucial concept in Bash scripting that allows us to manipulate variables in various ways. Within functions, the ability to expand and manipulate parameters dynamically is particularly useful. This section examines several parameter expansion methods, their syntax, and practical applications in functions.

Basic Parameter Expansion

The simplest form of parameter expansion involves retrieving the value of a variable. In the context of functions, this is frequently used to access function arguments or other variables.

```
function display_message {
    local message=$1
    echo ${message}
}
```

Executing display_message "Hello, World!" will output:

```
Hello, World!
```

Default Values

When dealing with function parameters, it might be necessary to provide default values. This can be achieved using the :- and := operators.

```
function greet_user {
    local name=${1:-"Guest"}
    echo "Welcome, ${name}"
}
```

Calling greet_user without any argument will result in:

```
Welcome, Guest
```

If an argument is provided, for instance, greet_user Alice, the output will be:

```
Welcome, Alice
```

Substring Extraction

Extracting substrings from parameters is another powerful tool. The syntax $variable:offset:length is used for substring extraction.

```
function extract_part {
    local string=$1
    local part=${string:2:4}
    echo ${part}
}
```

Executing extract_part "abcdefghijkl" will produce:

```
cdef
```

Length of a Variable

To obtain the length of a variable, the syntax $#variable is used. This is often useful for validation within functions.

```
function check_length {
    local input=$1
    local length=${#input}
    echo "The length of the input is ${length}"
}
```

If check_length "BashScripting" is called, the output will be:

```
The length of the input is 12
```

Pattern Replacement

Bash allows pattern replacement within variables using the $variable/-pattern/replacement syntax. This can be employed to modify function parameters.

```
function replace_char {
    local filename=$1
    local new_filename=${filename/.txt/.log}
    echo ${new_filename}
}
```

When replace_char "report.txt" is executed, it will give:

```
report.log
```

Removal of Prefix/Suffix

Removing prefixes or suffixes from variables can be particularly useful when dealing with file paths or URLs. To remove the shortest match of a prefix pattern, the syntax $variable#pattern is used, while the longest match is removed using $variable##pattern. Similarly, $variable%pattern removes the shortest match of a suffix pattern, and $variable%%pattern removes the longest match.

```
function strip_path {
    local path=$1
    local filename=${path##*/}
    echo ${filename}
}
```

Calling strip_path "/home/user/file.txt" results in:

```
file.txt
```

For suffix removal, consider the following function:

```
function strip_extension {
    local file=$1
```

```
    local name=${file%.txt}
    echo ${name}
}
```

Executing strip_extension "document.txt" yields:

```
document
```

Arithmetic Expansion

Arithmetic expansion allows for arithmetic operations within Bash scripts and functions using the $((expression)) syntax.

```
function add_numbers {
    local num1=$1
    local num2=$2
    local sum=$((num1 + num2))
    echo ${sum}
}
```

Executing add_numbers 5 10 provides:

```
15
```

Effective parameter expansion techniques enhance functionality and flexibility in Bash functions. It is essential to understand and utilize these expansions to write concise, efficient, and robust scripts.

6.10 Best Practices for Functions

To fully harness the power of functions in Bash scripting, adherence to established best practices is paramount. This not only ensures code readability and maintainability but also improves efficiency and reduces potential errors.

1. Naming Conventions Consistency in naming functions significantly enhances the readability of your codebase. Use descriptive names that clearly convey the function's purpose. It is recommended to use lowercase letters and separate words with underscores. This convention aligns with the standard Bash syntax.

```
# Example of a well-named function
calculate_sum() {
  local sum=0
  for number in "$@"; do
    sum=$((sum + number))
  done
```

```
  echo "$sum"
}
```

2. Function Documentation Documenting functions with comments ensures that other developers (and future you) can understand the function's purpose, parameters, and expected behavior. A good practice is to include a comment block before the function definition.

```
# Calculates the sum of all input parameters
# Usage: calculate_sum [num1 num2 ...]
# Example: calculate_sum 1 2 3
calculate_sum() {
  local sum=0
  for number in "$@"; do
    sum=$((sum + number))
  done
  echo "$sum"
}
```

3. Use of Local Variables Leveraging local variables within functions prevents variable name conflicts and unintended side effects in other parts of the script. Define variables within a function using the local keyword.

```
calculate_sum() {
  local sum=0
  local number
  for number in "$@"; do
    sum=$((sum + number))
  done
  echo "$sum"
}
```

4. Input Validation Validate the input parameters to ensure that functions handle unexpected or invalid data gracefully. This practice reduces runtime errors and enhances the function's robustness.

```
calculate_sum() {
  local sum=0
  local number

  for number in "$@"; do
    if ! [[ "$number" =~ ^-?[0-9]+$ ]]; then
      echo "Error: '$number' is not a valid integer"
      return 1
    fi
    sum=$((sum + number))
  done

  echo "$sum"
}
```

5. Return Values and Status Codes Bash functions can return values through output (using echo) and status codes. Utilize status codes to indicate success or error states, and use output for actual return data. A convention is to return 0 for success and non-zero for errors.

```
calculate_sum() {
  local sum=0
  local number

  for number in "$@"; do
    if ! [[ "$number" =~ ^-?[0-9]+$ ]]; then
      echo "Error: '$number' is not a valid integer" >&2
      return 1
    fi
    sum=$((sum + number))
  done

  echo "$sum"
  return 0
}
```

```
$ calculate_sum 1 2 3
6
$ calculate_sum 1 2 three
Error: 'three' is not a valid integer
```

6. Avoiding Side Effects Functions should be designed to perform specific tasks without causing side effects. This principle, also known as functional purity, ensures that functions do not modify global state or produce changes outside their scope unless explicitly necessary.

```
# Purity example
increment() {
  local value=$1
  value=$((value + 1))
  echo "$value"
}

# Impure example due to global variable modification
counter=0
increment_global() {
  counter=$((counter + 1))
}
```

7. Modularization and Reusability Break down complex tasks into smaller, reusable functions. This modular approach not only makes the script more readable but also allows functions to be reused in different parts of the script or across multiple scripts.

```
# Reusable functions
add() {
  echo $(( $1 + $2 ))
}

subtract() {
  echo $(( $1 - $2 ))
}

# Complex task using reusable functions
```

```
calculate() {
  local a=$1
  local b=$2
  local operation=$3

  case "$operation" in
    add)
      add "$a" "$b"
      ;;
    subtract)
      subtract "$a" "$b"
      ;;
    *)
      echo "Unknown operation"
      return 1
      ;;
  esac
}
```

8. Consistent Formatting and Indentation Adopt a consistent formatting style, including indentation, within functions. This consistency enhances readability and makes it easier to identify and troubleshoot code blocks. Use two or four spaces per indentation level.

```
calculate_product() {
    local product=1
    local number
    for number in "$@"; do
        product=$((product * number))
    done
    echo "$product"
}
```

9. Error Handling Implement robust error handling within functions to manage failures gracefully and provide meaningful feedback. This can be achieved using conditional checks and status codes.

```
calculate_product() {
    local product=1
    local number
    for number in "$@"; do
        if ! [[ "$number" =~ ^-?[0-9]+$ ]]; then
            echo "Error: '$number' is not a valid integer" >&2
            return 1
        fi
        product=$((product * number))
    done
    echo "$product"
}
```

```
$ calculate_product 2 3
6
$ calculate_product 2 three
Error: 'three' is not a valid integer
```

10. Function Testing Develop a set of test cases for functions to verify their behavior under various conditions. This practice, often referred to as unit testing, ensures that functions work as expected and facilitates future code changes and refactoring.

```
# Test cases for calculate_sum function
test_calculate_sum() {
    local result

    result=$(calculate_sum 1 2 3)
    if [[ "$result" != "6" ]]; then
        echo "Test Failed: Expected 6, got $result"
    else
        echo "Test Passed"
    fi

    result=$(calculate_sum -1 1)
    if [[ "$result" != "0" ]]; then
        echo "Test Failed: Expected 0, got $result"
    else
        echo "Test Passed"
    fi

    result=$(calculate_sum 1 two)
    if [[ "$result" != "Error: 'two' is not a valid integer" ]]; then
        echo "Test Failed: Expected input validation error"
    else
        echo "Test Passed"
    fi
}
```

By following these best practices, you will ensure that your Bash functions are reliable, maintainable, and efficient. These principles help reinforce a robust scripting discipline and facilitate collaboration among developers.

Chapter 7

Handling Input and Output

This chapter examines the methods for handling input and output in Bash scripting. It includes reading user input, using command line arguments, and redirecting standard input and output. The chapter also addresses handling errors with standard error, creating and reading files, using here documents for input, working with pipes, processing text with tools like awk, sed, and grep, and formatting output.

7.1 Introduction to Input and Output

In Bash scripting, effective handling of input and output is fundamental. Understanding how to read input from users, manage command line arguments, and control the redirection of standard streams is essential for composing robust and flexible scripts. This section delves into these core concepts, providing a comprehensive environment for mastering the intricacies of input and output in Bash.

To begin with, Bash scripts predominantly interact with three standard streams: standard input (stdin), standard output (stdout), and standard error (stderr). These are denoted by file descriptors 0, 1, and 2, respectively. The stdin represents the input stream from which the script reads data, the stdout is used to print output data, and the stderr is designated for error messages or diagnostics.

Each of these streams can be manipulated by redirection functionalities that allow us to control where the data comes from or goes to.

```
command > output.txt # Redirects stdout to a file
command < input.txt # Redirects stdin from a file
command 2> error.txt # Redirects stderr to a file
```

To illustrate the basic usage of these redirections, consider a script that reads from a file, processes the contents, and writes output to another file while logging possible errors.

```
#!/bin/bash
if [ ! -f "input.txt" ]; then
    echo "Input file not found!" 1>&2
    exit 1
fi

while read line; do
    echo $line | tr a-z A-Z >> output.txt
done < input.txt
```

In this example, the script first checks if the input.txt file exists. If not, it outputs an error message to stderr and exits with a status code of 1. If the file exists, it reads each line from stdin (redirected from input.txt), converts the text to uppercase, and appends the result to output.txt.

Besides redirection, piping, denoted by the | operator, is another powerful feature to channel the output of one command into the input of another. This mechanism enables the composition of complex command sequences.

```
cat input.txt | grep "pattern" | sort
```

In the above command, the output of cat input.txt is piped into grep "pattern", which filters lines containing the specified pattern, and then the filtered output is sorted.

Moreover, an advanced use of redirections involves merging standard streams. For instance, combining stderr and stdout to a single file can be achieved by:

```
command > output.txt 2>&1
```

This command redirects stdout to output.txt and then sends stderr to the same location as stdout.

Understanding these basic principles paves the way for more complex I/O operations, which we will explore in subsequent sections. The ability to flexibly manipulate input and output streams is a critical skill in efficient Bash scripting, making automation, data processing, and error handling more straightforward and manageable. Through practical examples and detailed explanations, this chapter equips you with the necessary tools to proficiently handle various I/O scenarios in your scripts.

7.2 Reading User Input

Reading user input in Bash scripts is fundamental for making scripts interactive. The read command allows the script to pause execution and wait for the user to enter data. The basic form of the read command is:

```
read variable_name
```

This command will prompt the user to input a value, which will be stored in the variable variable_name. For instance:

```
#!/bin/bash
echo "Please enter your name:"
read name
echo "Hello, $name!"
```

When this script is executed, it outputs a prompt message, waits for user input, and then stores the input in the name variable. The script will then greet the user by the name provided. Executing this script might produce the following interaction:

```
Please enter your name:
Alice
Hello, Alice!
```

Reading Multiple Values

The read command can also handle multiple values. When reading multiple values, the input is split based on the Internal Field Separator (IFS), which defaults to whitespace. For example:

```
#!/bin/bash
echo "Enter three values separated by spaces:"
read var1 var2 var3
echo "You entered: $var1, $var2, $var3"
```

An execution of this script would look like:

```
Enter three values separated by spaces:
apple orange banana
You entered: apple, orange, banana
```

Setting a Prompt

To enhance user experience, a prompt can be directly embedded using the -p option with the read command:

```
read -p "Enter your age: " age
echo "You are $age years old."
```

Executing the script would prompt:

```
Enter your age: 30
You are 30 years old.
```

Suppressing Input

For scenarios where user input must remain confidential, such as passwords, the -s option can be used to ensure that input is not displayed on the screen:

```
read -sp "Enter your password: " password
echo
echo "Password received."
```

An execution of this script would appear as:

```
Enter your password:
Password received.
```

Setting a Timeout

The -t option allows setting a timeout period for the user to respond. If the user doesn't input data within the specified time, the read command will return a non-zero exit status:

```
if read -t 5 -p "Enter your username (within 5 seconds): " username; then
    echo "Username: $username"
else
    echo "Time out. No input received."
fi
```

An interaction might produce:

```
Enter your username (within 5 seconds):
Time out. No input received.
```

Reading Input with Delimiters

Bash read can split input using custom delimiters by modifying the IFS variable directly:

```
IFS=',' read -p "Enter values separated by commas: " var1 var2 var3
echo "You entered: $var1, $var2, $var3"
```

If executed with the input:

```
Enter values separated by commas: red,green,blue
You entered: red, green, blue
```

Reading from a File

The read command can also fetch input from a file line by line. This is particularly useful for processing configuration files or data files:

```
#!/bin/bash
file="sample.txt"
while IFS= read -r line
do
  echo "Line: $line"
done < "$file"
```

Assuming sample.txt contains:

```
line1
line2
line3
```

Executing the script will produce:

```
Line: line1
Line: line2
Line: line3
```

Handling Errors

When using read in scripts, it is essential to handle potential errors such as empty input or invalid input formats. For instance, validating non-empty input:

```
read -p "Enter a non-empty value: " value
if [ -z "$value" ]; then
  echo "Error: No value entered."
  exit 1
fi
echo "Value: $value"
```

An execution might look like:

```
Enter a non-empty value:
Error: No value entered.
```

Combining Options

The read command supports combining multiple options to handle complex input. For example:

```
read -p "Enter username: " -s -t 10 username
echo
if [ -z "$username" ]; then
  echo "Error: no input or timeout."
else
  echo "Username: $username"
fi
```

An interaction might produce:

```
Enter username: error: no input or timeout.
```

These examples showcase the flexibility and power of the read command in Bash scripting. Consistent user input handling ensures that scripts are robust, secure, and user-friendly.

7.3 Using Command Line Arguments

Command line arguments provide a mechanism to pass parameters to a Bash script from the command line. These arguments are accessible within the script and can be employed to influence the script's behavior dynamically. This section elaborates on accessing, processing, and utilizing command line arguments effectively.

The arguments passed to a Bash script are stored in special positional parameters, namely $1, $2, $3, and so on. The first argument is accessible using $1, the second using $2, and this pattern continues for subsequent arguments. The total number of command line arguments is stored in the special variable $#, and the complete list of arguments is stored in $@ or $*.

```
#!/bin/bash
echo "First argument: $1"
echo "Second argument: $2"
echo "Total number of arguments: $#"
echo "All arguments: $@"
```

When executed with:

```
/path/to/script.sh arg1 arg2 arg3
```

The output will be:

```
First argument: arg1
Second argument: arg2
Total number of arguments: 3
All arguments: arg1 arg2 arg3
```

A critical aspect to recognize is the distinction between $@ and $*. Both variables include all the arguments, but their behavior differs based on quotation.

```
#!/bin/bash
echo "All arguments using \$*: $*"
echo "All arguments using \$@: $@"
echo "All arguments using \"\$*\": \"$*\""
echo "All arguments using \"\$@\": \"$@\""
```

When executed with:

```
/path/to/script.sh arg1 arg2 "arg 3"
```

The output will be:

```
All arguments using $*: arg1 arg2 arg 3
All arguments using $@: arg1 arg2 arg 3
All arguments using "$*": arg1 arg2 arg 3
All arguments using "$@": "arg1" "arg2" "arg 3"
```

The usage of double quotes distinguishes $@ from $*. Quoted $@ retains each argument as separate entries, preserving spaces within quoted strings. Conversely, quoted $* concatenates all arguments into a single string, with spaces separating the original arguments.

Additionally, scripts often require iterating over all passed arguments. This can be performed using a for loop.

```
#!/bin/bash
echo "Iterating over arguments:"
for arg in "$@"; do
    echo "$arg"
done
```

When executed with:

```
/path/to/script.sh arg1 arg2 "arg 3"
```

The output will be:

```
Iterating over arguments:
arg1
arg2
arg 3
```

Besides positional parameters, Bash also supports flags and options. Flags typically signify a boolean setting, while options may necessitate a value. Argument parsing utilities like getopts simplify the process of handling flags and options.

```
#!/bin/bash
while getopts "a:b:c" opt; do
  case $opt in
    a)
      echo "Option -a triggered, argument: $OPTARG"
      ;;
    b)
      echo "Option -b triggered, argument: $OPTARG"
      ;;
    c)
      echo "Option -c triggered"
      ;;
    \?)
      echo "Invalid option: -$OPTARG" >&2
      ;;
  esac
done
```

When executed with:

```
/path/to/script.sh -a foo -b bar -c
```

The output will be:

```
Option -a triggered, argument: foo
Option -b triggered, argument: bar
Option -c triggered
```

Here, getopts is employed to parse options. The string "a:b:c" specifies that options -a and -b require arguments, while -c does not. The colon (:) following a and b indicates their requirement for an argument, accessible via the $OPTARG variable.

Robust script design involves validating provided arguments to ensure they meet expected criteria. Conditional statements and regular expressions can be utilized for validation.

```
#!/bin/bash
if [[ -z "$1" ]]; then
  echo "No arguments supplied." >&2
  exit 1
fi

if ! [[ "$1" =~ ^[0-9]+$ ]]; then
  echo "First argument must be a number." >&2
  exit 1
fi

echo "Valid argument: $1"
```

When executed with:

```
/path/to/script.sh
```

The output will be:

```
No arguments supplied.
```

When executed with a non-numeric first argument:

```
/path/to/script.sh abc
```

The output will be:

```
First argument must be a number.
```

When executed with a numeric first argument:

```
/path/to/script.sh 123
```

The output will be:

```
Valid argument: 123
```

Effective handling of command line arguments enhances script functionality and flexibility, enabling dynamic parameterization and improved user interaction.

7.4 Redirecting Standard Input and Output

Redirecting standard input and output is a critical aspect of Bash scripting, allowing scripts to interact with the system and other commands more effectively. Bash provides several mechanisms for redirecting input and output: using operators to redirect standard input (stdin), standard output (stdout), and standard error (stderr).

Standard Output Redirection: The standard output, which is the default destination for the output of commands, can be redirected to a file or another command. The redirection operators for stdout include > and ».

```
# Redirect standard output to a file, overwriting the file
command > output.txt

# Redirect standard output to a file, appending to the file
command >> output.txt
```

When using the > operator, if the specified file already exists, its contents will be overwritten. The » operator, on the other hand, appends the output to the existing content of the file without overwriting.

Standard Input Redirection: Standard input, the default source of input for commands, can be redirected from a file rather than the keyboard. The redirection operator for stdin is <.

```
# Redirect standard input from a file
command < input.txt
```

This command instructs Bash to use the contents of input.txt as the input for command.

Standard Error Redirection: Standard error is the default destination for error messages. It can also be redirected to a file or another location using the 2> and 2» operators.

```
# Redirect standard error to a file, overwriting the file
command 2> error.log

# Redirect standard error to a file, appending to the file
command 2>> error.log
```

As with standard output, using 2> overwrites the specified file, while 2» appends to it.

Combining Redirections: Sometimes, it is necessary to redirect both stdout and stderr simultaneously. This can be achieved using the following syntax:

```
# Redirect both standard output and standard error to the same file
command > alloutput.txt 2>&1
```

In this example, 2>&1 instructs Bash to redirect stderr (file descriptor 2) to the same location as stdout (file descriptor 1). It is important to note the order of the redirections; reversing the order would result in different behavior.

Here Documents: A here document allows redirection of input directly within a script, providing a way to use multiline input. The syntax involves the « operator followed by a delimiter.

```
command <<EOF
line 1 of input
line 2 of input
EOF
```

In this example, everything between «EOF and the ending delimiter EOF is treated as the input for command. The delimiter can be any identifier, but EOF is commonly used.

Pipes: Pipes are used to pass the output of one command as input to another command. The pipe operator is |.

```
# Use a pipe to send output of one command to another
command1 | command2
```

command1 produces stdout which becomes stdin for command2.

Redirection of Both stdin and stdout: It is also possible to combine the redirection of both stdin and stdout in a single command. This is particularly useful for handling data streams.

```
# Redirect both standard input and standard output
command < input.txt > output.txt
```

By mastering the use of these redirection operators, you can effectively control the flow of information in your Bash scripts, achieving more complex and efficient interactions with the system and other commands.

7.5 Handling Errors with Standard Error

In Bash scripting, error handling is a crucial aspect of developing robust and reliable scripts. Standard error (stderr) is a specific stream used by programs to output error messages. By default, stderr is directed to the terminal, but it can be redirected, captured, or suppressed based on the needs of the script.

stderr is one of the three primary data streams:

- stdin (Standard Input) - File descriptor 0
- stdout (Standard Output) - File descriptor 1
- stderr (Standard Error) - File descriptor 2

To handle errors effectively, understanding how to manipulate stderr is essential.

Redirection of Standard Error

Redirection allows you to control where stderr is sent. This is particularly useful for logging errors separately from regular output or for debugging purposes.

```
command 2> errorfile.txt
```

In this example, any error messages produced by command are redirected to errorfile.txt. The 2> syntax specifically redirects stderr.

Similarly, you can append errors to a file rather than overwriting it:

```
command 2>> errorfile.txt
```

To redirect both stdout and stderr to the same file, you can use:

```
command > outputfile.txt 2>&1
```

Here, 2>&1 directs stderr (file descriptor 2) to the same location as stdout (file descriptor 1). Thus, both streams are combined into outputfile.txt.

Suppressing Errors

There are instances where it is desirable to ignore errors. This can be achieved by redirecting stderr to /dev/null, a special file that discards all data written to it.

```
command 2> /dev/null
```

This approach is useful when you are certain that the errors are not critical, and you want to keep the script's output clean.

Capturing Errors in Variables

Capturing error messages in variables allows finer control over error handling within scripts. Using process substitution, you can achieve this efficiently.

```
error_message=$(command 2>&1 > /dev/null)
```

In this case, command executes, and its error output is captured into the variable error_message, while its standard output is discarded.

Checking Exit Status

Apart from handling the error messages, it is essential to check the exit status of commands. The exit status provides another layer of error handling. A non-zero exit status indicates that an error occurred.

Here is an example demonstrating the use of the exit status:

```
command
if [ $? -ne 0 ]; then
    echo "An error occurred. Exit status: $?"
fi
```

In this script, $? holds the exit status of the last executed command. If it is not zero, an error message is printed.

Example: Comprehensive Error Handling in a Script

Consider a script that processes files and requires comprehensive error handling. The script will log errors and notify the user if any operation fails.

```
#!/bin/bash

log_error() {
    local errmsg="$1"
    echo "[$(date)] ERROR: $errmsg" >> error.log
}

process_file() {
    local filename="$1"
    if [ ! -f "$filename" ]; then
        log_error "File $filename not found"
        return 1
    fi

    # Simulate file processing
    if ! grep "keyword" "$filename" > /dev/null 2>&1; then
        log_error "Keyword not found in $filename"
        return 1
    fi

    echo "$filename processed successfully"
    return 0
}

for file in "$@"; then
    if ! process_file "$file"; then
        echo "Failed to process $file"
    fi
done
```

In this example, the log_error function logs errors with a timestamp. The process_file function checks if the file exists and if it contains the keyword. Errors are logged and handled appropriately, and the script processes each file passed as an argument, providing feedback on failures.

Handling errors effectively using stderr ensures that your Bash scripts are more reliable and easier to debug.

7.6 Creating and Reading Files

File handling is an essential aspect of Bash scripting, enabling scripts to store data persistently, process files dynamically, and retrieve information. This section delves into the mechanisms available in Bash for creating and reading files, ensuring that you can seamlessly integrate these operations into your scripts.

Creating files in Bash can be accomplished through various methods, each suited to different use cases. The simplest method to create a file is by using the touch command:

```
touch filename.txt
```

This command creates an empty file named filename.txt if it does not already exist. If the file exists, touch updates the file's timestamp to the current time.

Another common method for creating files involves using redirection. By redirecting the output of a command to a file, you can both create the file and write initial content to it. The redirection operator > creates a new file or truncates an existing file before writing to it:

```
echo "Hello, World!" > hello.txt
```

This command creates a file named hello.txt and writes the string "Hello, World!" to it. If hello.txt already exists, its content is replaced.

To append data to an existing file, the append redirection operator » is used:

```
echo "Appending this line." >> hello.txt
```

This adds the line "Appending this line." to the end of hello.txt without altering its existing content.

Reading files can be performed using several built-in Bash commands. The cat command reads and outputs the entire content of a file:

```
cat filename.txt
```

While cat is effective for displaying short files, it is less suitable for handling large files. For large files, less or more provide better control:

```
less largefile.txt
more largefile.txt
```

Both commands paginate the output, letting you navigate the file content interactively.

In scripts, reading the content of a file line by line is often necessary. The while loop, combined with read, provides an efficient way to accomplish this:

```
while IFS= read -r line
do
    echo "$line"
done < filename.txt
```

Here, IFS= ensures that leading and trailing whitespaces are preserved, and -r prevents backslashes from escaping any characters. The done < filename.txt stanza specifies that input should be read from filename.txt.

Another method to read a file is using the mapfile command, which reads a file into an array:

```
mapfile -t array < filename.txt
```

The -t option removes the trailing newline from each line. After executing this command, array contains each line from filename.txt as individual elements.

For more advanced file manipulation, the awk and sed tools are indispensable. awk operates as a programming language for text processing, while sed is a stream editor primarily used for transforming text in a pipeline.

Suppose you want to extract and print the second column from a file data.txt, where columns are space-separated. You can achieve this with awk:

```
awk '{print $2}' data.txt
```

With sed, you can perform operations such as replacing all occurrences of a string. For example, to replace every instance of "foo" with "bar" in file.txt, do:

```
sed 's/foo/bar/g' file.txt
```

Files can also be processed using input redirection, which allows a script to read data directly from a file. For example, to count the number of lines in file.txt, you can use:

```
wc -l < file.txt
```

This is more efficient than cat file.txt | wc -l, as it avoids creating a subshell pipeline.

Employing these file handling techniques, your Bash scripts can manage file creation and reading tasks effectively, allowing for robust data processing and manipulation.

7.7 Using Here Documents for Input

Here Documents (often referred to as "heredoc") provide a way to pass multiple lines of text or input to a command in Bash scripting without requiring interactive user input or reading from a separate file. Heredocs are particularly useful for feeding input streams to commands or scripting blocks by embedding the input directly within the script. This section will explore the syntax and usage of Here Documents in detail, highlighting practical applications and potential pitfalls.

The basic syntax of a Here Document involves the use of « followed by a delimiter (an arbitrary word, often EOF). The starting delimiter (e.g., «EOF) marks the beginning of the Here Document, and input continues until the closing delimiter is encountered. The delimiter must be on a line by itself, without leading or trailing spaces.

```
#!/bin/bash
cat <<EOF
This is a simple example of a Here Document.
It allows multi-line strings to be passed to commands.
EOF
```

In this example, the cat command receives a multi-line string as its input directly from the Here Document. The text between «EOF and EOF is fed to cat, which then prints it to standard output.

Usage with Variables

Variables can be expanded within a Here Document, allowing for dynamic content generation. The expansion depends on whether quotes are used around the delimiter.

```
#!/bin/bash
name="Alice"
cat <<EOF
Hello, $name!
Welcome to the Bash scripting tutorial.
EOF
```

In the example above, the variable $name is expanded to "Alice" within the Here Document. If you want to prevent variable expansion and preserve the literal text, you can quote the delimiter.

```
#!/bin/bash
name="Bob"
cat <<"EOF"
Hello, $name!
This will prevent variable expansion.
EOF
```

Here, the $name variable remains unexpanded due to the quoted delimiter "EOF".

Leveraging Here Documents with Command Substitution

Here Documents can be combined with command substitution to dynamically generate input. This is useful when the input to a command depends on the output of other commands.

```
#!/bin/bash
directory_list=$(ls -l)
cat <<EOF
The contents of the current directory are:
$directory_list
EOF
```

The ls -l command's output is captured into directory_list and then incorporated into the Here Document.

Interaction with File Descriptors

By default, Here Documents use the standard input file descriptor (file descriptor 0). However, they can be redirected to other file descriptors as necessary.

```
#!/bin/bash
cat <<EOF 1>output.txt
This text will be written to output.txt.
EOF
```

In this example, the output of the Here Document is redirected to output.txt using file descriptor 1 (standard output).

Practical Applications

Heredocs are instrumental in situations requiring embedded multi-line input, such as configuration files, automated inputs to interactive scripts, and more complex scripts requiring structured input.

Creating Configuration Files

Here Documents can create configuration files with required parameters directly within a Bash script.

```
#!/bin/bash
config_file="config.cfg"
cat <<EOF >$config_file
[main]
user=admin
pass=secret
port=8080
EOF
```

This script generates a configuration file named config.cfg with predefined parameters.

SQL Queries

Here Documents simplify running multi-line SQL queries directly from a script without needing separate SQL files.

```
#!/bin/bash
database="mydb"
user="dbuser"
password="dbpass"
mysql -u $user -p$password $database <<EOF
SELECT * FROM users WHERE active=1;
EOF
```

The above script connects to a MySQL database and runs a multi-line SQL query to select active users.

Potential Pitfalls

While Here Documents are powerful, they require careful attention to syntax:

- The delimiter must not have any leading or trailing whitespace.
- Quoted delimiters disable variable expansion, which is crucial for dynamic content.
- Invisible characters, such as tabs or spaces at the end of the delimiter line, can disrupt the Here Document's termination.

Proper understanding and usage of Here Documents can remarkably enhance the clarity and functionality of complex Bash scripts, embedding multi-line inputs seamlessly.

7.8 Working with Pipes

In Bash scripting, pipes provide a powerful mechanism to chain commands together, allowing the output of one command to serve as the input to another. This section delves into the syntax, usage, and practical applications of pipes in Bash, enhancing the reader's ability to leverage this feature for efficient data processing and command execution.

The pipe operator in Bash is represented by the vertical bar character (|). When a pipe is used, it connects the standard output (stdout) of the command preceding the pipe to the standard input (stdin) of the command following the pipe. The basic syntax for using a pipe is as follows:

```
command1 | command2
```

In this example, command1 produces output that is directly fed into command2 as input. This chaining of commands is particularly useful for filtering and processing data streams in a streamlined manner.

Consider the following example where we use ls to list directory contents and then use grep to filter for files matching a specific pattern:

```
ls -l | grep 'pattern'
```

Here, the ls -l command lists the files and directories in the current working directory in long format. The output of ls -l is piped to grep, which filters the lines containing the specified pattern.

Pipes can be used with more complex command sequences, allowing for sophisticated data processing. For instance, let's assume we wish to count the number of text files in a directory. We can achieve this by combining ls, grep, and wc:

```
ls -1 | grep '\.txt\$' | wc -l
```

Breaking down this command:

- ls -1 lists the directory contents in a single column.
- The pipe | sends this output to grep 'txt$', which filters the list for entries ending with .txt.
- The subsequent pipe sends the filtered output to wc -l, which counts the number of lines, effectively counting the number of text files.

Pipes are not limited to linear chains of commands. They also facilitate more complex workflows involving multiple stages of processing. Consider a scenario where data needs to be sorted and then displayed with specific formatting. We can chain sort and awk in the following manner:

```
sort data.txt | awk '{printf "%-10s %s\n", \$1, \$2}'
```

In this example:

- sort data.txt sorts the contents of data.txt.

- The sorted data is passed to awk, which formats each line according to the specified printf format string.

Another powerful use of pipes is in conjunction with commands that themselves generate significant output. For example, combining ps with grep:

```
ps aux | grep 'bash'
```

Here:

- ps aux lists all running processes.
- The output is piped to grep 'bash', which filters the processes to show only those related to the bash shell.

Additionally, pipes can connect multiple tools to achieve desired outcomes swiftly. For example, to extract specific content from a file, sort it, and remove duplicates:

```
cat file.txt | cut -d',' -f2 | sort | uniq
```

Breaking down this sequence of commands:

- cat file.txt outputs the contents of file.txt.
- With the first pipe, |, this output is sent to cut -d',' -f2, which extracts the second field (assuming fields are comma-separated).
- The resulting data is sent to sort, which orders the lines.
- Finally, uniq removes consecutive duplicate lines, producing a list of unique entries.

Pipes are also pivotal in handling real-time data streams. For instance, monitoring log files dynamically:

```
tail -f /var/log/syslog | grep 'error'
```

In this scenario:

- tail -f /var/log/syslog continuously outputs new additions to /var/log/syslog.
- This live output is piped to grep 'error', filtering for lines containing the word error.

By integrating pipes into Bash scripts, users can create efficient, concise, and readable operations for a variety of tasks, from simple text processing to complex data manipulation workflows, improving both productivity and script performance.

7.9 Processing Text with awk, sed, and grep

awk, sed, and grep are powerful command-line utilities used to process and manipulate text in Bash scripting. These tools are widely employed due to their efficiency and flexibility in handling various text-processing tasks.

grep: The grep command is used to search for patterns in files or input provided to it. It uses regular expressions to match the patterns. The basic syntax is:

```
grep [options] pattern [file...]
```

For instance, to search for the word "error" in a log file, the following command can be used:

```
grep "error" logfile.txt
```

Commonly used grep options include:

- -i: Ignore case distinctions.
- -v: Invert the match, showing lines that do not match the pattern.
- -r: Recursively search directories.
- -n: Prefix each line of output with the line number in the file.

sed: The sed stream editor is utilized to perform basic text transformations on an input stream (a file or input from a pipeline). The most common use of sed is for regular expression-based find and replace operations. The basic syntax is:

```
sed [options] 'script' [file...]
```

To replace all occurrences of "foo" with "bar" in a file, the following command can be used:

```
sed 's/foo/bar/g' input.txt
```

Useful sed options:

- -e script: Add the script to the commands to be executed.
- -i[SUFFIX]: Edit files in place (makes a backup if SUFFIX is supplied).
- -n: Suppress automatic printing of pattern space.

awk: The awk programming language is used for pattern scanning and processing. It is highly versatile and can perform complex data extraction and reporting. The basic syntax is:

```
awk 'pattern { action }' [file...]
```

For example, to print the second column of a CSV file, where columns are separated by commas, the following command is used:

```
awk -F, '{print $2}' input.csv
```

Commonly used awk options and actions:

- -F fs: Specify the field separator fs.
- $n: References the n-th field in the current record.
- NR: Refers to the number of input records processed.
- OFS: Output field separator.

```
$ grep "error" logfile.txt
error: file not found
error: permission denied
```

Combining these tools within pipelines provides robust functionality for complex text processing tasks. For example:

```
grep "pattern" filename.txt | sed 's/old/new/g' | awk '{print $3, $5}'
```

This command pipeline searches for lines containing "pattern" in filename.txt, replaces "old" with "new," and then prints the third and fifth fields from the resulting lines.

These utilities excel in both performance and flexibility, empowering users to efficiently process and transform text data within Bash scripts.

7.10 Formatting Output

Formatting output in Bash scripts is an essential skill for producing clear and readable outputs. This section details various techniques for formatting output ranging from simple echo commands with escape sequences to more complex formatting with printf and text processing tools.

To produce structured and readable output from your Bash scripts, you can use several methods. The basic tool is the echo command, which prints text to the standard output. By default, echo appends a newline character to its output. You can suppress this behavior using the -n option.

```
echo -n "This is a line without a newline character at the end."
```

Special characters, such as newline (\n), tab (\t), and others can be included in the output of the echo command using escape sequences. To enable interpretation of these sequences, the -e option is used.

```
echo -e "Line one.\nLine two."
```

Another method for formatted output is the printf command, which provides greater control over the formatting. It allows specifying the format of the output, similar to the C printf() function. The general syntax is:

```
printf format-string [arguments...]
```

Here, the format-string specifies how to format the text, and arguments supply the data to be formatted. Common format specifiers include:

- %s - String
- %d - Decimal integer
- %f - Floating point number
- %x - Hexadecimal integer

The following example demonstrates the usage of printf for various data types:

```
name="Alice"
age=30
height=5.6

printf "Name: %s\nAge: %d\nHeight: %.1f\n" "$name" "$age" "$height"
```

```
Name: Alice
Age: 30
Height: 5.6
```

The awk tool also allows for powerful formatting capabilities, especially for structured text data like CSV files. For example, you can use awk to format columns of data neatly.

```
awk 'BEGIN { printf "%-10s %s\n", "Name", "Score" }
{ printf "%-10s %d\n", $1, $2 }' scores.txt
```

In the above example, awk is used to print a table with left-aligned names and scores. The %-10s specifier indicates a left-aligned string in a field of width 10.

Combining awk with the printf function inside a script enhances the output formatting significantly:

```
#!/bin/bash
echo "Generating formatted output..."
awk 'BEGIN {
    FS=","
    printf "%-12s %-12s %-12s\n", "First Name", "Last Name", "Score"
    printf "%-12s %-12s %-12s\n", "----------", "----------", "-----"
}
{
    printf "%-12s %-12s %-12d\n", $1, $2, $3
}' data.csv
```

The script above reads from data.csv, which could contain lines like John,Doe,85, and outputs a neatly formatted table.

Additionally, when working with text processing tools such as sed, you can format text by substituting patterns:

```
echo "Hello, World!" | sed 's/World/Bash/'
```

This example will replace World with Bash resulting in:

```
Hello, Bash!
```

In many cases, proper formatting of output is crucial for readability, especially when scripts are used for reporting or logging purposes. Enhancing readability could involve aligning columns, adjusting text spacing, and organizing data elements systematically.

Bash scripting provides a robust set of tools and commands for output formatting, enabling scripts to produce outputs that are both user-friendly and suitable for automated processing. With practice and understanding of commands like echo, printf, awk, and sed, you can create versatile scripts with precisely formatted outputs.

Chapter 8

Working with Files and Directories

This chapter provides detailed guidance on working with files and directories in Bash scripting. It covers basic file operations such as creating, reading, and writing files, navigating the filesystem, and managing permissions and ownership. Additionally, readers will learn about working with links, using wildcards for file operations, finding files, checking disk usage, archiving and compressing files, and automating file management tasks.

8.1 Introduction to Files and Directories

Understanding how to work with files and directories is a fundamental skill in Bash scripting. This section explores the core concepts required for effectively managing files and directories in a Unix-like operating system.

A file is an ordered collection of bytes with a specific meaning and structure, whereas a directory is a special type of file that contains references to other files or directories. Learning to distinguish between these two entities and how to manipulate them through Bash scripting is essential for automation and system administration.

File Types: In Unix-like systems, files can be of various types:

- Regular Files: These are the most common file types, containing user data, text, binary code, etc.
- Directory Files: These are special files that act as containers for other files and directories.
- Special Files: These include device files, named pipes, and sockets. Each serves a specific function in system operation.
- Symbolic Links: Also known as symlinks, these are references or shortcuts to another file or directory.

Paths: Files and directories can be accessed using paths, which can be:

- Absolute Path: A path that starts from the root directory and specifies the complete address of the file or directory.
- Relative Path: A path relative to the current working directory, not starting with a root.

For example:

```
# Absolute Path
/home/user/documents/report.txt

# Relative Path
documents/report.txt
```

Navigating the Filesystem: It's crucial to understand some basic commands for navigating the file system:

- pwd: Prints the current working directory.
- cd: Changes the current directory.
- ls: Lists the files and directories in the current directory.

Consider this sequence of commands:

```
# Print the current directory
pwd

# Change to /home/user/documents directory
cd /home/user/documents

# List the contents of the current directory
ls
```

Output:

```
/home/user
doc1.txt  doc2.txt  report.txt
```

Creating Files and Directories: You can create files and directories using the following commands:

- touch filename: Creates an empty file named filename.
- mkdir dirname: Creates a new directory named dirname.

```
# Creating a new file named example.txt
touch example.txt

# Creating a new directory named my\_directory
mkdir my_directory
```

Viewing Files: There are several commands to view the contents of a file:

- cat: Concatenates and displays file contents.
- less: Displays file contents one screen at a time.
- head: Displays the first part of a file.
- tail: Displays the last part of a file.

```
# Displaying contents of example.txt
cat example.txt

# Viewing the first 10 lines of example.txt
head example.txt

# Viewing the last 10 lines of example.txt
tail example.txt
```

Copying and Moving Files: These are basic file management operations:

- cp source destination: Copies a file from source to destination.
- mv source destination: Moves or renames a file from source to destination.

```
# Copy example.txt to backup.txt
cp example.txt backup.txt

# Move example.txt to /home/user/documents and rename it to new_example.txt
mv example.txt /home/user/documents/new_example.txt
```

Deleting Files and Directories: You can remove files and directories using these commands:

- rm filename: Removes a file.
- rmdir dirname: Removes an empty directory.
- rm -r dirname: Removes a directory and its contents recursively.

```
# Deleting the file example.txt
rm example.txt

# Removing an empty directory named my_directory
rmdir my_directory

# Removing a directory and its contents
rm -r my_directory
```

By comprehending these fundamental operations, you can effectively interact with the file system and manipulate files and directories as required.

8.2 Basic File Operations: Create, Read, Write

Working with files is an essential aspect of Bash scripting. This section will cover the fundamental operations you can perform on files, including creating, reading, and writing files. These operations form the basis of many scripting tasks, allowing for effective file manipulation and data handling.

- Creating files
- Reading files
- Writing to files

Creating a file in Bash can be done through various methods, with some of the most common being touch and redirection operators.

Creating a File with touch:

The touch command is used to create an empty file or update the timestamp of an existing file. The syntax for creating an empty file is straightforward:

```
touch filename.txt
```

To verify the creation of the file, you can use the ls command to list the files in the directory:

```
ls -l filename.txt
```

```
-rw-r--r-- 1 user user 0 Jan 1 00:00 filename.txt
```

Creating a File with Redirection:

Redirection operators can also create files. The >, », and < operators are critical in file manipulation.

Using the > operator, you can create a file or truncate it if it exists:

```
echo "Sample text" > newfile.txt
```

This command writes "Sample text" to newfile.txt, creating the file if it does not exist.

Reading a File:

Reading from a file in Bash can be accomplished using commands like cat, less, more, and head/tail. Each command has distinct features:

Using cat:

The cat command displays the file contents to the standard output:

```
cat filename.txt
```

If filename.txt contains "Sample text", the command output will be:

```
Sample text
```

Using less **and** more:

These commands are beneficial for reading large files. less allows backward navigation, while more does not.

```
less filename.txt
more filename.txt
```

Use the q key to quit less or more.

Using head **and** tail:

These commands display the beginning or the end of a file:

```
head filename.txt
tail filename.txt
```

For example, head -n 10 filename.txt prints the first 10 lines, and tail -n 10 filename.txt prints the last 10 lines.

Writing to a File:

Writing to a file can be performed using redirection or commands like echo and printf.

Using echo:

The echo command is simple for writing text:

```
echo "Appending text" >> filename.txt
```

This command appends "Appending text" to filename.txt.

Using printf:

The printf command provides formatted output:

```
printf "Formatted text: %d\n" 123 > filename.txt
```

This command writes "Formatted text: 123" to filename.txt.

Writing Multiple Lines with cat:

Another method to write multiple lines is using a here-document with cat:

```
cat << EOF > filename.txt
Line 1
Line 2
Line 3
EOF
```

This script writes three lines to filename.txt.

Understanding these basic operations forms the foundation of file manipulation in Bash scripting, enabling efficient data processing and automation tasks.

8.3 Navigating the Filesystem

In this section, we will delve into navigating the filesystem using Bash commands. Understanding how to effectively move through the filesystem is crucial for efficient file management and automation in Bash scripting.

pwd (Print Working Directory)
The pwd command outputs the absolute path of the current working

directory. This command is fundamental as it allows users to verify their current location within the filesystem.

```
pwd
```

Sample Output:

```
/home/user/documents
```

cd (Change Directory)
The cd command is used to change the current directory. Its usage can be specified with either relative or absolute paths.

Relative Path Example:

```
cd projects
```

Absolute Path Example:

```
cd /home/user/projects
```

To move up one level in the directory hierarchy, use:

```
cd ..
```

Navigating directly to the home directory can be done using:

```
cd ~
```

ls (List Directory Contents)
The ls command lists the contents of a directory. It has several options that provide additional information about files and directories.

Common usages:

```
ls
ls -l # Long listing format
ls -a # Include hidden files
ls -la # Long listing format including hidden files
```

Sample Output for ls -la:

```
drwxr-xr-x  2 user user 4096 Mar 10 10:00 .
drwxr-xr-x 18 user user 4096 Mar 10 09:59 ..
-rw-r--r--  1 user user   27 Mar 10 10:00 .hiddenfile
drwxr-xr-x  2 user user 4096 Mar 10 10:00 directory
-rw-r--r--  1 user user   29 Mar 10 10:00 file.txt
```

tree (Directory Tree)
The tree command displays directories and files in a tree-like format. This requires separate installation on some systems. It is useful for visualizing the hierarchical structure of the filesystem.

Using tree:

```
tree
```

Sample Output:

```
.
  directory
     file2.txt
  file1.txt
```

pushd and popd (Directory Stack)

The pushd command saves the current directory on a stack and then changes to a new directory. Conversely, the popd command returns to the directory at the top of the stack and removes it from the stack. These commands are beneficial for temporary navigation.

Example of using pushd and popd:

```
pushd /home/user/projects
# Perform operations in /home/user/projects
popd
# Return to the original directory
```

dirs Command

The dirs command displays the directory stack, showing the currently saved directories.

Using dirs:

```
dirs
```

Sample Output:

```
/home/user/projects /home/user
```

Combining Commands with the Directory Stack

Directory stack operations can be combined to perform more complex navigations. For example, switching between two directories without losing track of the initial directory can be efficiently managed.

Example:

```
pushd /home/user/projects
# Directory stack: /home/user/projects /home/user

pushd /home/user/documents
# Directory stack: /home/user/documents /home/user/projects /home/user

popd
# Directory stack: /home/user/projects /home/user

popd
# Directory stack: /home/user
```

This sequence ensures you are back at the starting directory after performing operations in multiple directories.

find Command for Directory Navigation
The find command is crucial for locating files and directories that meet specific criteria. This can streamline the process of identifying target directories or files for further operations.

Basic Usage:

```
find /path/to/search -name "pattern"
```

Sample Command to Find a Directory:

```
find /home/user -type d -name "projects"
```

Using these commands, one can navigate the filesystem efficiently, ensuring precise and controlled directory traversal. Combining cd, ls, pushd, popd, dirs, and find facilitates robust and flexible navigation scripts.

8.4 Managing Permissions and Ownership

Understanding and managing file permissions and ownership is crucial for effective file and directory management in a multi-user environment. Bash provides a comprehensive set of tools to manipulate these attributes. This section delves into the details of Unix file permissions, owners, and groups, enabling you to control access and maintain security over your files and directories.

File Permissions

Each file and directory has a set of permissions that determine who can read, write, or execute the file. These permissions are represented by a combination of symbols and are divided into three categories: the user (or owner), the group, and others. The command ls -l displays file permissions in the long listing format:

```
$ ls -l
total 8
-rw-r--r-- 1 user group 887 Jan 11 08:28 file1.txt
-rwxr-xr-x 1 user group 230 Jan 11 08:29 script.sh
```

In the output, the first set of ten characters represents the file type and permissions. For example, -rw-r–r– can be broken down as follows:

- The first character signifies the file type (e.g., - for a regular file, d for a directory).
- The next three characters denote the owner's permissions (e.g., rw- means read and write).
- The next three characters represent the group permissions (e.g., r– means read-only).
- The last three characters specify the permissions for others (e.g., r– means read-only).

Changing Permissions

The chmod command is used to change the permissions of a file or directory. Permissions can be modified using either symbolic or numeric modes.

Symbolic Mode:

In symbolic mode, you specify the desired changes using symbols:

```
$ chmod u+x file1.txt # Adds execute permission for the owner
$ chmod g-w script.sh # Removes write permission for the group
$ chmod o=r file1.txt # Sets read-only permission for others
```

- u represents the user (owner).
- g represents the group.
- o represents others.
- a represents all (user, group, and others).
- r stands for read.
- w stands for write.
- x stands for execute.

Numeric Mode:

Numeric (octal) mode uses three numbers to represent the permissions for user, group, and others. Each permission (read, write, execute) is assigned a value:

- r (read) = 4

- w (write) = 2
- x (execute) = 1

To set a file's permissions, combine these values. For example, 755 means read, write, and execute for the owner, and read and execute for the group and others:

```
$ chmod 755 script.sh # Sets permissions to rwxr-xr-x
```

Changing Ownership

Ownership of a file or directory determines who can change its permissions and attributes. The chown (change owner) command changes the user and/or group ownership:

```
$ chown user:group file1.txt # Changes the owner to 'user' and the group to 'group'
$ chown user file1.txt # Changes only the owner
$ chown :group file1.txt # Changes only the group
```

The chgrp command changes the group ownership:

```
$ chgrp group file1.txt # Changes the group to 'group'
```

Special Permission Bits

In addition to the standard read, write, and execute permissions, there are special permission bits that can be set on files and directories.

Setuid and Setgid:

The setuid and setgid bits elevate privileges for executing files or accessing directories:

- Setuid (set user ID) - If set on an executable file, it allows the file to be executed with the privileges of the file's owner.
- Setgid (set group ID) - If set on an executable file, it allows the file to be executed with the privileges of the file's group. If set on a directory, files created within that directory inherit the group ownership.

To set these bits:

```
$ chmod u+s file1.txt # Sets the setuid bit
$ chmod g+s file2.txt # Sets the setgid bit
```

Sticky Bit:

The sticky bit is used on directories to restrict file deletion:

- Only the file's owner, the directory's owner, or the superuser can delete or rename files in that directory.

To set the sticky bit:

```
$ chmod +t directory # Sets the sticky bit on the directory
```

Viewing and Modifying ACLs

Access Control Lists (ACLs) provide a more granular permission mechanism. They allow specific permissions to be set for individual users or groups beyond what traditional Unix permissions accommodate. To view ACLs, use the getfacl command:

```
$ getfacl file1.txt
```

To modify ACLs, use the setfacl command:

```
$ setfacl -m u:user:rwx file1.txt # Grants the user 'user' read, write, and execute
      permissions
$ setfacl -m g:group:rx file1.txt # Grants the group 'group' read and execute
      permissions
```

Understanding and managing permissions and ownership is instrumental in maintaining system security and proper access control. This section has covered the essentials of file permissions, ownership, and the use of special permission bits, providing you with foundational knowledge to manage files and directories effectively.

8.5 Working with Links: Hard Links and Soft Links

In the context of Unix-like operating systems, symbolic links (symlinks) and hard links provide different methods to reference files. They both serve as pointers to file data, but they operate through distinct mechanisms with unique implications on file management, storage, and behavior across various file operations. This section will elucidate the creation, utilization, and differences between hard links and soft links within Bash scripting, enabling the reader to effectively leverage these tools for enhanced file management.

Hard Links

A hard link is an additional directory entry for a file. Each hard link points directly to the inode (index node) of a file, allowing multiple directory entries to reference the same data on disk. This means that operations performed on any of these directory entries (hard links) affect the same underlying file data. A file is only truly deleted from the filesystem when the last hard link is removed, making hard links a powerful tool for preserving data integrity while allowing flexible access patterns.

To create a hard link, use the ln command with the source file followed by the target link name:

```
ln original_file hard_link
```

For example, creating a hard link named example_link for a file named example_file would look like this:

```
ln example_file example_link
```

Verification of the hard link creation can be accomplished using the ls command with the -l option, which shows that both files share the same inode number and have the same file size:

```
ls -li example_file example_link
```

```
1234567 -rw-r--r-- 2 user group 1024 Jan 1 12:00 example_file
1234567 -rw-r--r-- 2 user group 1024 Jan 1 12:00 example_link
```

Notably, the inode number (1234567 in this case) and the file size indicate that both example_file and example_link reference the same underlying data.

Restrictions of hard links include the inability to link directories (to prevent circular references that could disrupt the directory structure) and they must reside within the same filesystem. They offer benefits such as data redundancy without additional storage consumption and consistent data access across multiple link paths.

Soft Links

A soft link, also known as a symbolic link or symlink, is a special file that acts as a reference to another file or directory. Unlike hard links, soft links are separate file entries that contain a pathname reference to the original file. If the target file is moved, renamed, or deleted, the symlink becomes a dangling link, essentially a broken reference.

To create a soft link, use the ln command with the -s option:

```
ln -s target_file symlink
```

For example, creating a symlink named example_symlink for a file named example_file would be executed as:

```
ln -s example_file example_symlink
```

Verification of the symlink creation can be achieved by listing the files with the ls -l command:

```
ls -l example_file example_symlink
```

```
-rw-r--r-- 1 user group 1024 Jan 1 12:00 example_file
lrwxrwxrwx 1 user group   12 Jan 1 12:00 example_symlink -> example_file
```

The lrwxrwxrwx file type indicator shows that example_symlink is a symlink, pointing to example_file. Unlike hard links, symlinks can point to directories and cross filesystem boundaries, providing more flexibility in linking structures.

Operational Differences and Use Cases

- **Deletion Behavior:** Deleting a hard link does not affect the underlying data until all hard links are removed. Deleting a symlink leaves the original file intact but results in a broken link.
- **File Size Impact:** Hard links do not consume additional disk space for file data, while symlinks require a small amount for the link information.
- **Filesystem Location:** Hard links cannot cross filesystem boundaries; symlinks can reference files on different filesystems.
- **Directory Linking:** Hard links cannot link directories due to potential structural issues, but symlinks can.

These differences dictate their use in various scenarios. Hard links are suitable for robust data management within a single filesystem, offering data redundancy and simplified recovery mechanisms. Symlinks offer greater flexibility and organizational capabilities, suitable for user-friendly directory and file navigation across systems and filesystems.

Example Implementation

Consider a scenario where nightly backups are required. A hard link implementation can preserve snapshots without additional storage costs:

```
cp -al /source/directory /backup/directory_$(date +%Y%m%d)
```

This command uses cp with -a (archive mode) and -l (link files instead of copying) to create a directory of hard links as a backup snapshot, timestamped by the current date.

For symlinks, organizing a directory structure with symlinks pointing to configuration files can simplify management:

```
ln -s /etc/myconfig.conf ~/myconfig.conf
```

Here, myconfig.conf in the user's home directory is a symlink to the actual configuration file in /etc, allowing seamless access and modification from the home directory while maintaining the real file location.

Understanding and utilizing hard links and soft links effectively equips the user with powerful tools to manage files efficiently, leveraging the strengths and flexibility of each linking mechanism to optimize file operations and organization within the Bash scripting environment.

8.6 Using Wildcards for File Operations

Wildcards, also known as globbing patterns, are characters that represent unspecified characters in filenames and paths within the filesystem. They are extremely powerful in Bash scripting for performing file operations on multiple files or directories simultaneously without the need to handle each file individually. This section will explore the various types of wildcards, their usage, and examples illustrating their practical applications.

1. The Asterisk (*)

The asterisk wildcard (*) represents zero or more characters in a filename or directory name. It can match any combination of characters, making it a versatile tool in file operations.

Example:

```
# List all files in the current directory
ls *

# List all text files in the current directory
ls *.txt

# Copy all files with a prefix 'report' to the backup directory
cp report* /backup/
```

In the above example, report* will match any file starting with "report", such as report1.txt, report_final.pdf, and so on.

2. The Question Mark (?)

The question mark wildcard (?) represents a single character. It can be used to match filenames and directories with a specific number of characters or patterns.

Example:

```
# List all files with names of 4 characters in the current directory
ls ????

# Rename files with names starting with 'file' and a single character extension to '.bak'
for f in file?.txt; do mv \$f \${f%.txt}.bak; done
```

Here, file?.txt will match files like file1.txt or fileA.txt.

3. The Square Brackets ([ ])

Square brackets ([ ]) are used to match any single character from a set or range of characters specified within the brackets.

Examples:

```
# List files that start with 'photo' followed by a digit (0-9)
ls photo[0-9]*

# List files that end with '.jpeg' or '.jpg'
ls *.[jJ][pP][eE][gG]
```

In the second example, *.[jJ][pP][eE][gG] will match file.jpeg, image.JPG, and so on.

4. Using Ranges and Sets

Within the square brackets, a range of characters can be specified using a hyphen (-), and individual characters can be listed to match any one of them.

Examples:

```
# List files that start with 'doc' followed by any lowercase letter a-l
ls doc[a-l]*

# List files that start with 'note' and end with a digit or upper/lowercase letter from x-
    z
ls note*[x-zX-Z0-9]
```

5. Negating a Set

A caret (^) or exclamation mark (!) inside square brackets negates the set, matching any character not included in the specified range or set.

Examples:

```
# List files that do not start with 'a', 'b', or 'c'
ls [^abc]*

# List files that do not have a digit in their names
ls *[!0-9]*
```

6. Brace Expansion

Brace expansion is not a wildcard per se, but it is useful for creating multiple text strings or filenames in a concise manner. It generates patterns containing multiple combinations of specified elements.

Examples:

```
# Create directories named 'project1', 'project2', and 'project3'
mkdir project{1,2,3}

# List files with extensions .c, .h, and .cpp
ls *.{c,h,cpp}
```

Here, *.c,h,cpp will match any file ending in .c, .h, or .cpp.

Combining Wildcards for Powerful File Operations

Wildcards can be combined in a single command to execute more complex file operations efficiently.

Examples:

```
# List all JPEG files (case insensitive) starting with 'image' and having exactly one
    digit before the extension
ls image?[jJ][pP][eE][gG]

# Move all documents and images to the archive directory
mv *.{docx,pdf,jpg,jpeg,png} /archive/
```

In this section, we addressed the utility and flexibility of wildcards in Bash scripting for file operations. With these tools, one can perform complex tasks effortlessly by leveraging the power of pattern matching.

8.7 Finding Files with Find and Locate

Effective file management often necessitates locating specific files or directories within a complex hierarchical file system. The find and locate commands in Bash provide powerful tools for this purpose.

find is a versatile command that searches for files within a directory hierarchy based on a variety of conditions. The basic syntax of the find command is:

```
find [path...] [expression]
```

path specifies the directories to search. If omitted, find defaults to the current directory. expression includes options, tests, and actions that dictate the search behavior.

- -name pattern: Searches for files with names matching pattern. The pattern uses shell globbing characters.
- -type type: Searches for files of a specific type (e.g., f for regular files, d for directories).
- -mtime n: Searches for files modified n days ago. +n means more than n days, and -n means less than n days.
- -size n: Searches for files of size nc for bytes, k for kibibytes, M for mebibytes, etc.

Consider the following example that searches for all .txt files in the current directory, including its subdirectories:

```
find . -name "*.txt"
```

To find all directories named backup, you would use:

```
find / -type d -name "backup"
```

The find command's strengths lie in its intricate options. For instance, you can find all files over 100 MB modified within the last 7 days:

```
find / -type f -size +100M -mtime -7
```

Actions can also be performed on located files. For instance, to delete all .tmp files older than 30 days:

```
find / -type f -name "*.tmp" -mtime +30 -exec rm {} \;
```

Here, -exec allows the execution of a command on each located file, with {} serving as a placeholder for the file name.

On the other hand, locate offers a faster method of finding files by searching an indexed database, typically updated daily by updatedb. The basic syntax of the locate command is:

```
locate [options] pattern
```

pattern matches parts of file paths. The primary advantage of locate over find is speed, though it may not find files created after the last database update.

To find files named myfile.txt, use:

```
locate myfile.txt
```

The locate command can also filter results, such as displaying only exact file names using the -b option (basename matching):

```
locate -b '\myfile.txt'
```

To continuously obtain the most accurate results, periodically update the locate database:

```
updatedb
```

Both find and locate facilitate flexible and efficient file search within a filesystem. While find provides detailed and real-time file searches with substantial control over the search criteria and actions, locate complements it by offering quicker results for frequent, simple searches, leveraging its indexed database. Employing these commands masterfully enhances filesystem navigation and file management efficiency.

8.8 Checking Disk Usage and File Sizes

Disk utilization is a fundamental aspect of system management. Monitoring and analyzing disk usage helps ensure optimal performance and prevents unexpected outages due to disk space shortage. This section delves into various Bash commands and techniques to efficiently check disk usage and file sizes within a filesystem.

df (disk free) is a command-line utility to display the amount of available disk space for file systems, while du (disk usage) shows the amount of disk space used by files and directories.

```
$ df -h
```

The -h flag stands for human-readable format. It converts the sizes into a readable format (KB, MB, GB).

```
Filesystem      Size  Used Avail Use% Mounted on
/dev/sda1        50G   20G   28G  42% /
tmpfs           500M     0  500M   0% /dev/shm
```

For more detailed information, including filesystem types and inode usage, the -T and -i options respectively can be used:

```
$ df -Th
```

```
Filesystem     Type      Size  Used Avail Use% Mounted on
/dev/sda1      ext4       50G   20G   28G  42% /
tmpfs          tmpfs     500M     0  500M   0% /dev/shm
```

```
$ df -i
```

```
Filesystem      Inodes  IUsed   IFree IUse% Mounted on
/dev/sda1      3276800 200000 3076800    6% /
tmpfs           128000      1  127999    1% /dev/shm
```

Switching focus to file and directory sizes, the du command provides insights into disk space usage directed towards specific files or directories. By default, du lists the disk usage in blocks.

```
$ du -sh /home/username
```

The -s flag summarizes the total disk usage of the specified directory, while -h renders the output in a human-readable format.

```
45G /home/username
```

To understand disk usage recursively, itemizing each directory and file, utilize:

```
$ du -ah /home/username
```

```
2.2M    /home/username/document.pdf
660K    /home/username/notes.txt
45G     /home/username
```

When dealing with larger filesystems, it is efficient to sort the output by size. This can be achieved through piping the du output to sort. To detect the largest directories, use:

```
$ du -ah /home/username | sort -rh | head -n 10
```

The -r flag in sort reverses the order so the largest sizes appear first, while head limits the output to the top 10 results.

File size and type can also be analyzed using the stat command, which provides detail beyond just size.

```
$ stat /home/username/document.pdf
```

```
  File: '/home/username/document.pdf'
  Size: 2345678     Blocks: 4584       IO Block: 4096   regular file
Device: 802h/2050d Inode: 12345678    Links: 1
Access: (0644/-rw-r--r--)  Uid: 1000  Gid: 1000
Access: 2023-09-30 10:05:14.000000000 +0000
Modify: 2023-09-29 18:03:02.000000000 +0000
Change: 2023-09-29 18:03:02.000000000 +0000
 Birth: -
```

For continuous monitoring, the watch command is useful. Combine it with df or du to automatically repeat the command:

```
$ watch -n 60 df -h
```

This command re-executes the df -h command every 60 seconds, helping keep track of disk usage in real-time.

Understanding and using these commands ensures effective disk space management, aiding in avoiding potential system interruptions.

8.9 Archiving and Compressing Files

Archiving and compressing files is a crucial skill in managing storage space and transferring files efficiently. This section discusses how to create archives, compress the archives, and extract them using bash commands. We will examine tools such as tar, gzip, and bzip2, along with the syntax for their most common operations.

The tar command is useful for creating an archive file that contains a collection of files and directories. To create a tar archive, you can use the c (create) option, along with the v (verbose) and f (file) options:

```
tar cvf archive_name.tar file1 file2 dir1
```

In this example, archive_name.tar is the name of the archive file created, while file1, file2, and dir1 are the files and directory included in the archive.

To list the contents of an existing tar archive without extracting it, use the following command:

```
tar tvf archive_name.tar
```

To extract the contents of a tar archive, use the x (extract) option:

```
tar xvf archive_name.tar
```

To create a tarball that is compressed using gzip, an additional option z should be used:

```
tar czvf archive_name.tar.gz file1 file2 dir1
```

The resulting file, archive_name.tar.gz, is both archived and compressed. To extract this file, the same process is used with the z option included:

```
tar xzvf archive_name.tar.gz
```

Alternatively, if bzip2 compression is desired, use the j option:

```
tar cjvf archive_name.tar.bz2 file1 file2 dir1
```

Extracting a bzip2 compressed archive involves the j option as well:

```
tar xjvf archive_name.tar.bz2
```

Standalone usage of gzip and bzip2 is also possible. For instance, to compress a file using gzip, the command is:

```
gzip filename
```

This command replaces filename with filename.gz. To decompress it, use:

```
gunzip filename.gz
```

Similarly, to compress a file using bzip2, use:

```
bzip2 filename
```

This results in filename.bz2. For decompression, use:

```
bunzip2 filename.bz2
```

When working with compression algorithms, understanding the balance between speed and compression ratio is essential. gzip generally offers faster compression and decompression at the cost of a slightly lower compression ratio compared to bzip2.

To automate the process of archiving and compressing files using a Bash script, you can incorporate conditional logic to determine the appropriate method. Below is an example script using the algorithm2e package:

Algorithm 2: Automate Archive and Compression

```
Input: Directory name to archive and compress
Output: Compressed archive file
inputDir=$1;
if [ -z "$inputDir" ] then
    echo "No directory specified.";
    exit 1;
end
archiveName="$inputDir.tar";
if [ ! -d "$inputDir" ] then
    echo "Directory does not exist.";
    exit 1;
end
tar -cvf "$archiveName" "$inputDir";
if [$? -eq 0] then
    echo "Directory archived successfully.";
    gzip "$archiveName";
    if [$? -eq 0] then
        echo "Archive compressed successfully.";
    end
    else
        echo "Compression failed.";
    end
end
else
    echo "Archiving failed.";
end
```

This script automates the process of checking if a directory exists, creating a tar archive and subsequently compressing it using gzip. The use of tar and gzip ensures that directories and files are efficiently managed in a single, compressed file.

Understanding the commands and scripts to archive and compress files lays the groundwork for more advanced operations such as scheduling backups and transferring large datasets efficiently. This knowledge equips practitioners with the tools needed to manage system resources effectively.

8.10 Automating File Management Tasks

Automating repetitive file management tasks can significantly enhance productivity and ensure consistency in file operations. Bash scripting provides robust capabilities to automate these tasks efficiently. In this section, we will explore automating various file management tasks such as batch renaming, moving files based on patterns, scheduled backups, and log rotation.

Batch Renaming Files

Renaming multiple files manually can be tedious. Bash scripting allows us to automate this process using loops and text manipulation commands. Consider a directory with multiple files having a common prefix that needs to be changed. The following script demonstrates how to rename files with a given pattern:

```
#!/bin/bash

# Define the prefix to be replaced and the new prefix
old_prefix="old_"
new_prefix="new_"

# Loop through all files with the old prefix
for file in ${old_prefix}*; do
    # Extract the filename without the prefix
    new_name=${file#${old_prefix}}
    # Rename the file with the new prefix
    mv "${file}" "${new_prefix}${new_name}"
done
```

old_prefix and new_prefix are defined to store the prefixes. The script iterates over files matching old_prefix*, removes the old_prefix using parameter expansion, and renames the file with the new_prefix.

Moving Files Based on Patterns

Automating file movement based on patterns can help organize files systematically. For example, moving all log files from different directories into one archive directory:

```
#!/bin/bash

# Define the source directories and the target directory
source_dirs=("/var/log" "/home/user/logs")
target_dir="/archive/logs"

# Create the target directory if it doesn't exist
mkdir -p "${target_dir}"

# Loop through each source directory
for dir in "${source_dirs[@]}"; do
    # Find and move all .log files to the target directory
```

```
    find "${dir}" -type f -name "*.log" -exec mv {} "${target_dir}" \;
done
```

The script defines source_dirs and target_dir, then iterates through each source directory, finding and moving all .log files to the target directory using the find command with the -exec option.

Scheduled Backups

Cron jobs offer a method to schedule regular file backups. A sample script to back up a user's home directory to an external drive might look like this:

```
#!/bin/bash

# Define the source and backup directories
source_dir="/home/user"
backup_dir="/mnt/backup"

# Get current date for the backup file name
current_date=$(date +"%Y-%m-%d")

# Create the backup directory if it doesn't exist
mkdir -p "${backup_dir}"

# Archive and compress the home directory
tar -czf "${backup_dir}/backup_${current_date}.tar.gz" -C "${source_dir}" .
```

To schedule this script, use the crontab command:

```
crontab -e
```

Add the following line to run the script every day at 2 AM:

```
0 2 * * * /path/to/backup_script.sh
```

Log Rotation

Log files can grow significantly over time, consuming disk space. Automating log rotation prevents this. Below is a simple script for rotating log files:

```
#!/bin/bash

# Define the log file and backup directory
log_file="/var/log/myapp.log"
backup_dir="/var/log/myapp_backup"

# Create the backup directory if it doesn't exist
mkdir -p "${backup_dir}"

# Get current date for backup file name
current_date=$(date +"%Y-%m-%d")

# Rotate the log file
cp "${log_file}" "${backup_dir}/myapp_${current_date}.log"
> "${log_file}"
```

The script creates a backup of the log file with the current date appended to the file name and then truncates the original log file using a redirection.

Automating file management tasks not only helps in maintaining organized file systems but also significantly reduces the time and effort required for manual file operations. Understanding these automation techniques enhances scripting capabilities and ensures efficient management of resources.

Chapter 9

Advanced Scripting Techniques

This chapter explores advanced scripting techniques in Bash, including the use of regular expressions, text manipulation with awk and sed, and working with JSON and XML data. It covers parsing command line options with getopt and getopts, concurrent execution and job control, and using traps to handle signals. The chapter also includes creating menus and dialog boxes, interfacing with databases, and writing secure scripts.

9.1 Introduction to Advanced Scripting

In the domain of Bash scripting, basic scripting constructs such as loops, conditionals, and functions facilitate the development of simple scripts. However, to create more robust, efficient, and powerful scripts, one must delve into advanced scripting techniques. This section provides an overview of various advanced topics that will be elaborated upon in subsequent sections, establishing a foundation for mastering Bash scripting at a higher level.

Bash scripts often require sophisticated control over text processing, data manipulation, and system interaction. Proficiency in employing regular expressions, leveraging text processing tools like awk and sed, and handling structured data formats such as JSON and XML is crucial for efficient scripting. Additionally, scripts often need to parse command-line arguments, execute tasks concurrently, and handle system signals gracefully.

Regular expressions play a vital role in text processing. They enable scripts to search, match, and manipulate text patterns within files or streams. A solid understanding of regular expression syntax and usage is essential for performing complex text manipulations efficiently. Consider the following example, which demonstrates the use of regular expressions to find and replace text in a file:

```
#!/bin/bash
# Replace all instances of 'foo' with 'bar' in the input file
sed -e 's/foo/bar/g' input.txt > output.txt
```

The awk and sed utilities further enhance text processing capabilities. awk is a powerful language designed for pattern scanning and processing. It is particularly useful for extracting and reporting data from structured text files. Similarly, sed, a stream editor, excels at performing basic text transformations in a streamlined manner. For instance, to extract the second field from each line of a comma-separated file, one might use:

```
#!/bin/bash
# Extract the second field from a CSV file
awk -F, '{print $2}' input.csv
```

Handling structured data formats such as JSON and XML requires specialized tools. jq is a lightweight and flexible command-line JSON processor. It enables querying and manipulating JSON data in a concise manner. For example, to extract the value of a specific key from a JSON file:

```
#!/bin/bash
# Extract the value associated with the 'name' key from JSON file
jq '.name' input.json
```

Command-line option parsing is another critical aspect of advanced scripting. It allows scripts to handle various user inputs and options gracefully, enhancing usability. The getopt and getopts utilities provide mechanisms for parsing command-line arguments. getopt is more powerful and flexible, supporting long options and complex option specifications. Here is an example of using getopt to handle options:

```
#!/bin/bash
# Parse command line options
OPTS=$(getopt -o ab:c:: --long option1,option2: -- "$@")
eval set -- "$OPTS"
while true; do
```

```
  case "$1" in
    -a|--option1)
      echo "Option 1 selected"
      shift
      ;;
    -b|--option2)
      if [ -n "$2" ]; then
        echo "Option 2 with value: $2"
        shift 2
      else
        echo "Option 2 without value"
        shift
      fi
      ;;
    --)
      break
      ;;
    *)
      echo "Invalid option"
      exit 1
      ;;
  esac
done
```

Concurrent execution and job control allow scripts to perform multiple tasks simultaneously, improving efficiency and performance. Utilizing background processes and managing them effectively with job control commands can significantly enhance script functionality. For example, to run multiple tasks concurrently:

```
#!/bin/bash
# Run three commands concurrently
command1 &
command2 &
command3 &
wait
```

Signal handling enhances the robustness of scripts by enabling them to respond to system signals appropriately. The trap command in Bash can capture signals like SIGINT or SIGTERM and execute specified actions. This is particularly useful for cleaning up resources or performing specific tasks upon termination. Consider the following example, which traps the SIGINT signal:

```
#!/bin/bash
# Trap SIGINT (Ctrl+C) and perform cleanup
trap 'echo "Caught SIGINT, performing cleanup"; cleanup_function' SIGINT

cleanup_function() {
  # Cleanup tasks here
  echo "Cleaning up"
  exit 0
}

# Simulate long-running process
echo "Running... Press Ctrl+C to trigger trap."
```

```
sleep 30
```

Creating interactive menus and dialog boxes enhances user interaction and script usability. Tools like dialog can create text-based user interfaces for input and choice selections. An example of a simple menu using dialog:

```
#!/bin/bash
# Display a menu using dialog and capture the user's choice
CHOICE=$(dialog --menu "Choose an option" 15 50 3 1 "Option 1" 2 "Option 2" 3 "
    Option 3" 3>&1 1>&2 2>&3 3>&-)
echo "You chose: $CHOICE"
```

Scripts often need to interface with databases to query, insert, update, or delete data. Utilizing command-line database clients like mysql or psql enables script interaction with databases. For instance, using mysql to execute a query:

```
#!/bin/bash
# Execute a SQL query using mysql client
mysql -u username -p'password' -e 'SELECT * FROM database.table'
```

Security is paramount in scripting, especially when handling sensitive data or performing privileged operations. Best practices include validating inputs, using secure communication methods, and minimizing the use of file permissions. An example of secure script execution:

```
#!/bin/bash
# Securely read input and validate it
read -p "Enter username: " username
if [[ ! "$username" =~ ^[a-zA-Z0-9_]+$ ]]; then
  echo "Invalid username."
  exit 1
fi
echo "Username is valid."
```

This section has outlined various advanced scripting topics that will be explored in greater detail in subsequent sections. Mastering these techniques will equip you with the necessary skills to create powerful, efficient, and secure Bash scripts.

9.2 Using Regular Expressions

Regular expressions (regex) are a powerful tool for pattern matching and string manipulation, essential skills in advanced Bash scripting. This section delves into regex syntax and application, providing practical examples to illustrate concepts.

Regular expressions consist of characters and metacharacters, defining search patterns. These patterns can be used with various Bash utilities like grep, sed, and awk.

Basic Syntax:

- . : Matches any single character.
- * : Matches zero or more occurrences of the preceding element.
- + : Matches one or more occurrences of the preceding element.
- ? : Matches zero or one occurrence of the preceding element.
- \ : Escapes a special character.
- [] : Matches any one of the enclosed characters.
- [^] : Matches any character not in the enclosed set.
- {} : Specifies a specific number of occurrences.
- () : Groups regex patterns.
- | : Acts as a logical OR.
- ^ : Anchors the match at the start of a string.
- $: Anchors the match at the end of a string.

Example 1: Basic Pattern Matching

Use grep to find lines containing the word error.

```
grep "error" logfile.txt
```

```
Line 1: critical error at module XYZ
Line 7: minor error reported
```

Example 2: Using Wildcards with . and *

Match lines with any character preceding error.

```
grep ".error" logfile.txt
```

```
Line 1: critical error at module XYZ
Line 2: system error encountered
Line 7: minor error reported
```

Example 3: Matching Multiple Instances

Match lines where error appears one or more times.

```
grep "error+" logfile.txt
```

```
Line 1: critical error at module XYZ
Line 7: minor error reported
```

Advanced Examples:

Example 4: Using Character Sets

Match lines containing any digits.

```
grep "[0-9]" logfile.txt
```

```
Line 5: reboot scheduled at 3:00
```

Example 5: Multiple Patterns with |

Match lines containing either success or failure.

```
grep "success\|failure" logfile.txt
```

```
Line 3: login success
Line 4: login failure due to incorrect password
```

Example 6: Grouping Expressions

Match lines where either critical or minor precedes error.

```
grep "\(critical\|minor\) error" logfile.txt
```

```
Line 1: critical error at module XYZ
Line 7: minor error reported
```

Example 7: Anchors

Match lines starting with the word error.

```
grep "^error" logfile.txt
```

```
<No matches found>
```

Match lines ending with error.

```
grep "error$" logfile.txt
```

```
Line 2: system error encountered
```

Practical Applications:

Using regex in sed to perform substitutions:

```
sed 's/error/issue/g' logfile.txt
```

```
Original: Line 1: critical error at module XYZ
Modified: Line 1: critical issue at module XYZ
```

Using regex in awk for pattern matching:

```
awk '/error/ {print \$0}' logfile.txt
```

```
Line 1: critical error at module XYZ
Line 2: system error encountered
Line 7: minor error reported
```

Understanding regular expressions enhances your ability to manipulate and analyze text data efficiently. Employing regex with Bash utilities enables the development of powerful, flexible scripts.

9.3 Manipulating Text with awk and sed

awk and sed are two powerful command-line utilities utilized for text processing in Bash scripting. These tools are essential for efficiently editing, filtering, and transforming text data, making them ideal for handling large datasets, configuration files, and log files.

sed (stream editor) is designed to perform basic text transformations on an input stream (a file or input from a pipeline). It can execute various operations such as substitution, insertion, deletion, and more complex manipulations based on patterns.

```
# Basic substitution syntax in sed:
sed 's/original/replacement/' filename

# Example: Replace "cat" with "dog" in file.txt
sed 's/cat/dog/' file.txt
```

The command above reads file.txt, and substitutes the first occurrence of the string cat with dog in each line.

To replace all occurrences of a pattern within each line:

```
# Replace all occurrences of "foo" with "bar" in file.txt
sed 's/foo/bar/g' file.txt
```

The g flag at the end of the substitute command ensures global substitution within each line.

sed can also handle more complex substitutions by using regular expressions.

```
# Replace only words that start with "A" and end with "e" with "Found".
sed 's/\<A[^ ][^ ]*e\>/Found/g' file.txt
```

Here, the regex \<A[^][^]*e\> matches words beginning with 'A' and ending with 'e', and substitutes them with the word Found.

To delete lines matching a specific pattern:

```
# Delete lines containing the word "delete".
sed '/delete/d' file.txt
```

awk, on the other hand, is more of a full-fledged programming language designed for text processing. It processes files line by line, with each line divided into fields based on a delimiter (default is whitespace). It is ideal for extracting, reporting, and editing structured text files.

```
# Basic awk syntax to print a specific field and line number:
awk '{print NR, $1}' filename

# Example: Print line numbers along with the first field from file.txt
awk '{print NR, $1}' file.txt
```

The above command prints the line number (NR) and the first field ($1) of each line from file.txt.

To print specific fields separated by a custom delimiter:

```
# Example: File with colon-separated fields, print first and third fields.
awk -F':' '{print $1, $3}' file.txt
```

The -F option defines the field separator, in this case, a colon.

awk also provides the ability to filter lines based on patterns and apply various actions.

```
# Example: Print lines where the second field is greater than 100.
awk '$2 > 100' file.txt
```

This command prints all lines of file.txt where the second field is greater than 100.

Combining sed and awk with other command-line tools enhances the flexibility and power of text processing in Bash scripts. For instance, consider a scenario to extract and transform specific columns from a CSV-like file.

```
# Example: Extract data from csvfile.csv, replace "N/A" with "0" in second column.
awk -F',' '{print $1, $2}' csvfile.csv | sed 's/N\/A/0/'
```

Here, awk extracts the first and second columns, and then sed replaces N/A with 0 in the output stream.

Understanding and mastering sed and awk will significantly enhance the efficiency and capability of your text manipulation tasks within scripts. Utilizing these tools allows for the creation of powerful, yet concise scripts tailored to handle complex text processing requirements with precision.

9.4 Working with JSON and XML Data

Bash scripts often need to interact with structured data formats such as JSON and XML. Both formats are ubiquitous in modern computing for configuration files, web services, and APIs. This section delves into the methods and tools available for handling JSON and XML data within Bash scripts, offering practical examples and explanations.

JSON (JavaScript Object Notation) is a lightweight data-interchange format that is easy to read and write for humans and easy to parse and generate for machines. XML (eXtensible Markup Language) is another flexible data format that is widely used for both document storage and data interchange.

Parsing JSON Data

To parse JSON data, we can utilize tools like jq. jq is a powerful command-line JSON processor that allows you to filter, extract, and manipulate JSON data.

```
sudo apt-get install jq
```

Consider the following JSON data stored in a file named data.json:

```
{
    "name": "John Doe",
```

```
    "age": 30,
    "address": {
        "street": "123 Main St",
        "city": "Anytown",
        "state": "CA",
        "postalCode": "12345"
    },
    "phoneNumbers": [
        {"type": "home", "number": "555-555-5555"},
        {"type": "fax", "number": "555-555-5556"}
    ]
}
```

To extract the name and age, use the following jq command:

```
jq '.name, .age' data.json
```

```
"John Doe"
30
```

To access nested elements, such as the street address, use the dot notation:

```
jq '.address.street' data.json
```

```
"123 Main St"
```

To retrieve all phone numbers, iterate over the array:

```
jq '.phoneNumbers[] | {type, number}' data.json
```

```
{
  "type": "home",
  "number": "555-555-5555"
}
{
  "type": "fax",
  "number": "555-555-5556"
}
```

Parsing XML Data

For parsing XML data, the xmlstarlet tool is commonly used. xmlstarlet is a command-line utility that can parse, query, and transform XML data.

Install xmlstarlet using:

```
sudo apt-get install xmlstarlet
```

Consider the following XML data stored in a file named data.xml:

```
<person>
    <name>John Doe</name>
    <age>30</age>
    <address>
        <street>123 Main St</street>
        <city>Anytown</city>
```

```
        <state>CA</state>
        <postalCode>12345</postalCode>
    </address>
    <phoneNumbers>
        <phone>
            <type>home</type>
            <number>555-555-5555</number>
        </phone>
        <phone>
            <type>fax</type>
            <number>555-555-5556</number>
        </phone>
    </phoneNumbers>
</person>
```

To extract the name and age, use the following xmlstarlet command:

```
xmlstarlet sel -t -m "//person" -v "name" -n -v "age" data.xml
```

```
John Doe
30
```

To access nested elements such as the street address:

```
xmlstarlet sel -t -m "//address" -v "street" data.xml
```

```
123 Main St
```

To retrieve all phone numbers, iterate over the relevant XML nodes:

```
xmlstarlet sel -t -m "//phoneNumbers/phone" -v "type" -o ": " -v "number" -n data.
    xml
```

```
home: 555-555-5555
fax: 555-555-5556
```

Transforming Data Formats

Occasionally, it becomes necessary to convert data between JSON and XML formats. Various tools and programming languages, such as Python, can facilitate this transformation. For example, a Python script can be used to convert JSON to XML and vice versa.

Install Python packages for JSON and XML manipulation:

```
pip install json2xml xmltodict
```

Example Python script to convert JSON to XML:

```
import json
from json2xml import json2xml
from json2xml.utils import readfromstring

json_data = '''
{
    "name": "John Doe",
```

```
    "age": 30,
    "address": {
        "street": "123 Main St",
        "city": "Anytown",
        "state": "CA",
        "postalCode": "12345"
    },
    "phoneNumbers": [
        {"type": "home", "number": "555-555-5555"},
        {"type": "fax", "number": "555-555-5556"}
    ]
}
'''

data_dict = readfromstring(json_data)
xml_data = json2xml.Json2xml(data_dict).to_xml()
print(xml_data)
```

Running the above script would produce:


```
<?xml version="1.0" ?>
<root>
  <name>John Doe</name>
  <age>30</age>
  <address>
    <street>123 Main St</street>
    <city>Anytown</city>
    <state>CA</state>
    <postalCode>12345</postalCode>
  </address>
  <phoneNumbers>
    <phoneNumbers>
      <type>home</type>
      <number>555-555-5555</number>
    </phoneNumbers>
    <phoneNumbers>
      <type>fax</type>
      <number>555-555-5556</number>
    </phoneNumbers>
  </phoneNumbers>
</root>
```


These tools and commands offer powerful ways to efficiently handle JSON and XML data within Bash scripts, enabling sophisticated data processing and automation workflows.

9.5 Parsing Command Line Options with getopt and getopts

Parsing command line options in a robust and user-friendly way is essential for creating effective Bash scripts. Two primary tools for this purpose are getopt and getopts. Each provides a method for handling options and arguments, although they have distinct differences in functionality and use cases. This section delves into the nuances and applications of getopt and getopts, providing comprehensive examples to illustrate their usage.

getopt is an external program that can be used to break up options and arguments in command lines for easy parsing by shell scripts. It supports long options, making it very flexible. However, the syntax and complexity can be a bit intimidating for beginners.

Here is an example demonstrating the use of getopt:

```
#!/bin/bash

# Define options
OPTIONS=h,help,v,version
LONGOPTIONS=help,version

# Parse the command line arguments
PARSED=$(getopt --options $OPTIONS --longoptions $LONGOPTIONS --name "$0"
    -- "$@")
if [[ $? -ne 0 ]]; then
    # getopt has complained about wrong arguments to stdout
    exit 2
fi

# Use eval with set command to handle the parsed options
eval set -- "$PARSED"

# Process the parsed options
while true; do
    case "$1" in
        -h|--help)
            echo "Usage: $0 [--help|-h] [--version|-v]"
            shift
            ;;
        -v|--version)
            echo "Version 1.0"
            shift
            ;;
        --)
            shift
            break
            ;;
        *)
            echo "Unknown option: $1"
            exit 3
            ;;
    esac
done
```

This script defines both short and long options and demonstrates parsing them using getopt. It uses eval and set to reprocess the arguments so that they are handled correctly in a while loop.

```
$ ./myscript.sh --help
Usage: ./myscript.sh [--help|-h] [--version|-v]

$ ./myscript.sh -v
Version 1.0
```

On the other hand, getopts is a built-in shell function that parses short options only, not long options. It is simpler to use for scripts that do not require long options. Here is an example of how to use getopts:

```
#!/bin/bash

# Initialize options
while getopts "hv" opt; do
    case ${opt} in
        h )
            echo "Usage: $0 [-h] [-v]"
            ;;
        v )
            echo "Version 1.0"
            ;;
        \? )
            echo "Invalid option: $OPTARG" 1>&2
            ;;
    esac
done
```

This example shows a simple use of getopts to handle -h and -v options. One key limitation of getopts is its inability to handle long options directly.

```
$ ./myscript.sh -h
Usage: ./myscript.sh [-h] [-v]

$ ./myscript.sh -v
Version 1.0
```

One way to extend getopts to handle long options is by preprocessing the command line arguments. The following script illustrates an approach where long options are translated into short options before passing them to getopts:

```
#!/bin/bash

# Preprocess long options to short options
for arg in "$@"; do
    shift
    case "$arg" in
        "--help") set -- "$@" "-h" ;;
        "--version") set -- "$@" "-v" ;;
        *) set -- "$@" "$arg" ;;
    esac
done

# Initialize options
while getopts "hv" opt; do
    case ${opt} in
        h )
            echo "Usage: $0 [-h] [-v]"
```

```
            ;;
        v )
            echo "Version 1.0"
            ;;
        \? )
            echo "Invalid option: $OPTARG" 1>&2
            ;;
    esac
done
shift $((OPTIND -1))
```

This script re-parses the arguments, converting long options to their short equivalents and then using getopts to handle them. This approach allows for the flexibility of getopt-style long options while utilizing the simpler getopts function for parsing.

Effective command line option parsing distinguishes professional, user-friendly scripts from rudimentary ones. Whether you leverage getopt for its extensive feature set or prefer getopts for its simplicity, understanding and appropriately applying these tools is a critical skill in advanced Bash scripting.

9.6 Concurrent Execution and Job Control

Concurrent execution and job control are crucial aspects in advanced Bash scripting that enable the efficient handling of multitasking operations within scripts. By utilizing concurrent execution, multiple tasks can be performed simultaneously, leading to optimized performance and resource utilization. Job control mechanisms allow for the management of these concurrent tasks, providing the ability to pause, resume, and terminate processes as needed.

To initiate concurrent execution, Bash provides the ability to run commands in the background using the ampersand (&) operator.

```
#!/bin/bash
# Start long-running task in the background
./long_running_task.sh &
# Execute another task concurrently
./other_task.sh
```

In this example, the long_running_task.sh script is executed in the background, allowing the other_task.sh script to run concurrently.

The job control mechanisms in Bash include job management commands such as jobs, fg, bg, and kill. These commands provide a means to oversee and manipulate jobs that are running in the background.

```
#!/bin/bash
# Running background jobs
./job1.sh &
./job2.sh &
# List all jobs
jobs
# Bring the first job to the foreground
fg %1
# Send the second job to the background
bg %2
# Terminate the first job
kill %1
```

The jobs command lists all jobs with their statuses, the fg command brings a job to the foreground, the bg command sends a job to the background, and the kill command terminates a job.

Job control signals in Bash, such as SIGTSTP (Stop), SIGCONT (Continue), and SIGTERM (Terminate), play a pivotal role in job management. These signals can be sent to jobs using the kill command:

```
#!/bin/bash
# Start a long-running process in the background
./process.sh &
# List jobs to get job number
jobs
# Stop the job
kill -s SIGTSTP %1
# Resume the job
kill -s SIGCONT %1
# Terminate the job
kill -s SIGTERM %1
```

Bash allows for advanced job control by incorporating wait commands and process substitution patterns. The wait command is utilized to pause script execution until the specified background job completes, facilitating synchronization:

```
#!/bin/bash
# Start background jobs
./task1.sh &
task1_pid=$!
./task2.sh &
task2_pid=$!
# Wait until both jobs are finished
wait $task1_pid
wait $task2_pid
echo "Both tasks completed."
```

In this script, $! stores the process ID (PID) of the last executed background job, which is then used with wait to ensure that the script waits for both tasks to complete before proceeding.

Process substitution enables more sophisticated parallel processing by redirecting the output of background processes as inputs to other commands. In the following example, the outputs of two background processes are merged using cat:

```
#!/bin/bash
# Process substitution to merge outputs
cat <(./process1.sh) <(./process2.sh)
```

This form of redirection provides a streamlined method for concurrent processing and output combination.

The use of named pipes (FIFOs) can also facilitate communication between concurrently running processes. Named pipes allow processes to communicate through file descriptors, enhancing the level of control over inter-process communication:

```
#!/bin/bash
# Create a named pipe
mkfifo mypipe
# Read from the pipe in the background
cat mypipe &
# Write to the pipe
echo "Hello, World!" > mypipe
# Clean up
rm mypipe
```

Named pipes act as conduits that support concurrent read and write operations, streamlining data flow between processes.

Combining these techniques with effective job control can lead to robust, efficient Bash scripts capable of handling complex multitasking scenarios.

9.7 Using Traps to Handle Signals

In Bash, the trap command allows the execution of a specified command when the shell receives specific signals. This capability is crucial for writing robust and resilient scripts that can handle unexpected interruptions, clean up resources, and maintain a controlled execution flow. Understanding and effectively using trap can significantly enhance the reliability and stability of your Bash scripts.

A signal is a limited form of inter-process communication used to notify a process that an event has occurred. Some common signals include SIGINT (interrupt, typically initiated by pressing Ctrl+C), SIGTERM (termination), and SIGHUP (hangup, dropped connection).

The trap syntax is:

```
trap 'command' signal1 signal2 ...
```

For example, to handle SIGINT and SIGTERM, you can define a cleanup function and use trap to execute this function upon receiving these signals:

```
#!/bin/bash

cleanup() {
    echo "Cleaning up temporary files..."
    rm -f /tmp/mytempfile
    echo "Cleanup complete."
}

trap 'cleanup' SIGINT SIGTERM

# Simulate a lengthy process
echo "Starting a long-running process..."
sleep 1000
echo "Process completed."
```

When the script is running, pressing Ctrl+C initiates SIGINT, leading to the execution of the cleanup function. This ensures that temporary files or other resources are properly handled, even if the script is interrupted.

Ignoring Signals

In certain situations, you might want to ignore specific signals to prevent the default action from occurring. This can be accomplished by providing an empty string to the trap command:

```
trap '' SIGINT
```

This command instructs the shell to ignore SIGINT. It is essential to use this capability cautiously, as ignoring critical signals might result in runaway processes or an inability to terminate the script normally.

Restoring Default Signal Behavior

To restore the default action for a signal, use the - character:

```
trap - SIGINT
```

This is particularly useful when you want to temporarily modify the signal handling behavior and then revert to the default.

Advanced Example: Signal Handling in a Loop

Consider a more advanced scenario where a script needs to handle signals while performing operations in a loop, such as processing multiple files. The following example demonstrates trapping SIGINT to cleanly exit the loop and perform necessary cleanup:

```
#!/bin/bash

cleanup() {
    echo "Caught SIGINT. Cleaning up..."
    rm -f /tmp/mytempfile
    echo "Cleanup complete."
    exit 1
}

trap 'cleanup' SIGINT

echo "Processing files..."

for file in /path/to/files/*; do
    echo "Processing $file..."
    # Simulate processing with a sleep
    sleep 2
done

echo "All files processed successfully."
```

Pressing Ctrl+C during the loop interrupts the processing, triggering the cleanup function, which ensures that temporary files are removed and the script exits gracefully.

Combining Multiple Commands

When multiple commands need to be executed upon receiving a signal, they can be combined in a single trap command by separating them with a semicolon:

```
trap 'echo "Signal received. Performing cleanup..."; rm -f /tmp/mytempfile; echo "Done
    ."' SIGINT SIGTERM
```

This approach allows for more complex signal handling logic to be incorporated straightforwardly.

Using Exit Traps

Bash also supports an EXIT trap that triggers when the script exits, whether it reaches the end, an explicit exit command is invoked, or a fatal error occurs. This can be useful for ensuring cleanup tasks are performed regardless of how the script terminates:

```
#!/bin/bash

cleanup() {
    echo "Script exiting. Performing cleanup..."
    rm -f /tmp/mytempfile
    echo "Cleanup complete."
}

trap 'cleanup' EXIT
```

```
# Simulate some operations
echo "Creating temporary file..."
touch /tmp/mytempfile

# Intentionally cause an error to demonstrate EXIT trap
nonexistent-command

echo "This message will not be printed due to the error above."
```

The nonexistent-command fails, causing the script to exit prematurely. The cleanup function is executed because of the EXIT trap, ensuring that temporary files are removed.

Understanding and implementing signal trapping with trap enhances a script's robustness, ensuring that resources are managed correctly and operations are terminated gracefully. This consideration is paramount when dealing with long-running processes, temporary files, or systems where stability and reliability are crucial.

9.8 Creating Menus and Dialog Boxes

Creating menus and dialog boxes in Bash scripts enhances user interaction by providing a structured way to capture user inputs. These interfaces simplify complex scripts, making them more user-friendly. This section delves into building text-based menus with the select command, using whiptail and dialog utilities to create graphical dialog boxes, and handling user selections efficiently.

The select command in Bash provides a straightforward method to create simple, text-based menus. Here's how to create a menu using select:

```
PS3='Please enter your choice: '
options=("Option 1" "Option 2" "Option 3" "Quit")
select opt in "${options[@]}"
do
    case $opt in
        "Option 1")
            echo "You chose choice 1"
            ;;
        "Option 2")
            echo "You chose choice 2"
            ;;
        "Option 3")
            echo "You chose choice 3"
            ;;
        "Quit")
            break
            ;;
        *) echo "invalid option $REPLY";;
    esac
```

```
done
```

In this example, the PS3 variable sets the prompt, and the select command iterates over the array ${options[@]}, presenting the user with a numbered list of choices. The case statement within the do loop determines the action based on the user's selection.

In scenarios requiring more sophisticated dialog boxes, the whiptail and dialog utilities provide extensive options for creating graphical interfaces. To begin, ensure these utilities are installed. On Debian-based systems, you can install them using:

```
sudo apt-get install whiptail dialog
```

whiptail is a lightweight utility for creating dialog boxes. Below is an example of a whiptail menu:

```
whiptail --title "Menu Example" --menu "Choose an option" 15 60 4 \
"1" "Option 1" \
"2" "Option 2" \
"3" "Option 3" \
"4" "Quit" 2>menu_choice.txt

choice=$(<menu_choice.txt)
case $choice in
    1)
        echo "You chose option 1"
        ;;
    2)
        echo "You chose option 2"
        ;;
    3)
        echo "You chose option 3"
        ;;
    4)
        echo "Quit selected"
        ;;
    *)
        echo "Invalid choice"
        ;;
esac
```

The whiptail command here specifies a menu with a title, dimensions, and menu options. The selected choice is stored in the file menu_choice.txt, which is then read to take appropriate action.

dialog provides similar functionality with potential for even richer interactions. Here is a basic example for creating a dialog menu:

```
dialog --title "Menu Example" --menu "Choose an option" 15 60 4 \
"1" "Option 1" \
"2" "Option 2" \
"3" "Option 3" \
"4" "Quit" 2>menu_choice.txt
```

```
choice=$(<menu_choice.txt)
case $choice in
    1)
        echo "You chose option 1"
        ;;
    2)
        echo "You chose option 2"
        ;;
    3)
        echo "You chose option 3"
        ;;
    4)
        echo "Quit selected"
        ;;
    *)
        echo "Invalid choice"
        ;;
esac
```

In addition to menus, both whiptail and dialog support various dialog types, such as input boxes, message boxes, and checklists. An example of an input box using whiptail is as follows:

```
whiptail --title "Input Box Example" --inputbox "Enter some text" 10 60 2>input.txt
input=$(<input.txt)
echo "You entered: $input"
```

Similarly, an input box created with dialog can be defined as:

```
dialog --title "Input Box Example" --inputbox "Enter some text" 10 60 2>input.txt
input=$(<input.txt)
echo "You entered: $input"
```

These examples demonstrate how user-provided input can be captured and utilized within a script.

To efficiently handle user selections and inputs, implement error handling and validation mechanisms. For instance, ensure that the user's input meets the expected format or range. One way to achieve this is by looping the input prompt until valid data is received.

```
while true; do
    whiptail --title "Input Box Example" --inputbox "Enter a number between 1 and 10
        " 10 60 2>input.txt
    input=$(<input.txt)
    if [[ $input =~ ^[1-9]$|^10$ ]]; then
        echo "Valid input: $input"
        break
    else
        whiptail --title "Error" --msgbox "Invalid input. Please enter a number between
            1 and 10." 10 60
    fi
done
```

This approach ensures that the script only processes valid data, thereby reducing the likelihood of runtime errors or unexpected behavior.

The integration of menus and dialog boxes significantly enhances the usability of Bash scripts, making them accessible to users with varying levels of technical proficiency. By leveraging tools like select, whiptail, and dialog, complex scripts can be transformed into intuitive applications that guide users through tasks with ease.

9.9 Interfacing with Databases

Interfacing with databases is a crucial aspect of advanced Bash scripting, enabling scripts to interact with structured data efficiently. Bash scripts can interface with various types of databases, including relational (such as MySQL, PostgreSQL) and NoSQL (such as MongoDB). This section focuses on techniques to connect, query, and manipulate databases using Bash.

To begin, establishing a connection to a database is essential. Many databases provide command-line tools to facilitate these connections. For instance, mysql for MySQL, psql for PostgreSQL, and mongo for MongoDB.

```
#!/bin/bash
# Define database connection parameters
DB_HOST="localhost"
DB_USER="user"
DB_PASS="password"
DB_NAME="database"

# Establish connection and execute a simple query
mysql -h $DB_HOST -u $DB_USER -p$DB_PASS -D $DB_NAME -e "SHOW
    TABLES;"
```

The listed script connects to a MySQL database and executes a simple query to list all tables. The connection parameters such as DB_HOST, DB_USER, DB_PASS, and DB_NAME represent the database's host, username, password, and database name, respectively. The -e option executes the subsequent SQL command.

Similarly, connection to a PostgreSQL database can be achieved with the following script:

```
#!/bin/bash
# Define database connection parameters
DB_HOST="localhost"
DB_USER="user"
DB_PASS="password"
DB_NAME="database"
```

```
# Establish connection and execute a simple query
PGPASSWORD=$DB_PASS psql -h $DB_HOST -U $DB_USER -d $DB_NAME -c "
    \dt"
```

This PostgreSQL script connects to the specified database and lists all tables using the \dt command. The PGPASSWORD environment variable is used to supply the database password.

Interfacing with MongoDB follows a similar pattern using the mongo command:

```
#!/bin/bash
# Define database connection parameters
DB_HOST="localhost"
DB_PORT="27017"
DB_USER="user"
DB_PASS="password"
DB_NAME="database"

# Establish connection and execute a simple query
mongo --host $DB_HOST --port $DB_PORT -u $DB_USER -p $DB_PASS --
    authenticationDatabase $DB_NAME --eval "db.getCollectionNames()"
```

This script connects to a MongoDB database and retrieves a list of all collections using the db.getCollectionNames() command.

Queries and data manipulation are pivotal in database interactions. For example, inserting, updating, and deleting records in a relational database can be accomplished using SQL commands. Below is a script to insert a record into a MySQL database:

```
#!/bin/bash
# Define database connection parameters
DB_HOST="localhost"
DB_USER="user"
DB_PASS="password"
DB_NAME="database"

# SQL insert statement
SQL_INSERT="INSERT INTO tablename (column1, column2) VALUES ('value1', '
    value2');"

# Execute insert statement
mysql -h $DB_HOST -u $DB_USER -p$DB_PASS -D $DB_NAME -e "
    $SQL_INSERT"
```

This script demonstrates how to construct an SQL INSERT statement and execute it through the mysql command. Similarly, updates and deletes can be implemented as shown below:

```
#!/bin/bash
# Define database connection parameters
DB_HOST="localhost"
DB_USER="user"
DB_PASS="password"
```

```
DB_NAME="database"

# SQL update statement
SQL_UPDATE="UPDATE tablename SET column1='newvalue' WHERE column2='
    value2';"

# Execute update statement
mysql -h $DB_HOST -u $DB_USER -p$DB_PASS -D $DB_NAME -e "
    $SQL_UPDATE"
```

```
#!/bin/bash
# Define database connection parameters
DB_HOST="localhost"
DB_USER="user"
DB_PASS="password"
DB_NAME="database"

# SQL delete statement
SQL_DELETE="DELETE FROM tablename WHERE column1='value1';"

# Execute delete statement
mysql -h $DB_HOST -u $DB_USER -p$DB_PASS -D $DB_NAME -e "
    $SQL_DELETE"
```

Handling query results in Bash requires capturing the output and processing it. To capture and iterate through rows returned from a query, the `while read` loop is beneficial:

```
#!/bin/bash
# Define database connection parameters
DB_HOST="localhost"
DB_USER="user"
DB_PASS="password"
DB_NAME="database"

# Query to execute
QUERY="SELECT column1, column2 FROM tablename;"

# Execute query and process results
mysql -h $DB_HOST -u $DB_USER -p$DB_PASS -D $DB_NAME -e "$QUERY" |
    while read -r column1 column2
do
  echo "Column 1: $column1, Column 2: $column2"
done
```

This script captures the results of a SELECT query and iterates through each row, echoing the values of `column1` and `column2`.

In practice, Bash scripts can interface with databases to automate various data-driven tasks, offering a robust mechanism to handle operations typically managed by higher-level programming languages. The use of command-line tools and scripting constructs enables efficient interaction with databases, leveraging the power of shell scripting for database management.

9.10 Writing Secure Scripts

When writing Bash scripts, ensuring security is paramount. This section delves into practices and techniques to minimize vulnerabilities and protect scripts from malicious exploitation. Emphasis is placed on input validation, privilege management, secure handling of sensitive data, and avoiding common pitfalls that may lead to security breaches.

Input Validation

Input validation is crucial to prevent unexpected or harmful data from influencing script behavior. A script should always validate and sanitize inputs to ensure they conform to expected formats and values before use.

Consider validating an integer input:

```
read -p "Enter a number: " input
if ! [[ "$input" =~ ^[0-9]+$ ]]; then
  echo "Invalid input: Please enter a numeric value."
  exit 1
fi
```

In this example, the script reads user input and uses a regular expression to verify that the input consists solely of digits. If the input fails validation, an error message is displayed, and the script terminates.

Privilege Management

Running scripts with the least privilege necessary is fundamental to security. Consider the principle of least privilege, where a script should execute with minimal permissions needed to accomplish its task, reducing the potential impact of an exploit.

For instance, avoid running scripts with root privileges unless absolutely necessary. Usage of sudo should be restricted and monitored. If privileged operations are required, carefully scope and control these segments:

```
if [[ $EUID -eq 0 ]]; then
  echo "This script must not be run as root. Exiting."
  exit 1
fi
```

In the above code, the script checks if it is being executed with root privileges and exits if so, promoting safer execution practices.

Secure Handling of Sensitive Data

Sensitive data, such as passwords or API keys, should be handled with care to prevent exposure. Avoid hardcoding sensitive information directly into scripts. Environment variables offer a more secure alternative, and sensitive outputs should leverage secure, temporary storage:

```
# Export sensitive data as environment variables
export API_KEY="your_api_key_here"

# Use within the script without hardcoding
curl -H "Authorization: Bearer $API_KEY" https://api.example.com/data
```

Always ensure sensitive information is accessed and passed securely. For example, use 'read -s' for hidden input input when prompting for passwords:

```
read -s -p "Enter your password: " password
echo
```

The '-s' flag ensures the input is not displayed on the terminal, reducing the risk of shoulder surfing attacks.

Avoiding Common Pitfalls

Several common pitfalls can inadvertently introduce security vulnerabilities. Below, a range of potential issues and corresponding mitigation strategies are discussed.

Command Injection

Command injection occurs when untrusted input is concatenated into a shell command without proper sanitization. This can lead to arbitrary command execution:

```
# Vulnerable to command injection
rm -rf /usr/local/$1
```

Mitigate this vulnerability by avoiding direct incorporation of user input into shell commands. Instead, leverage Bash's built-in mechanisms like arrays and parameter substitution, or use validated input:

```
# Use an array for executing commands
args=("$1")
if [[ -d "/usr/local/${args[0]}" && ( ${args[0]} != *"/"* ) ]]; then
  rm -rf "/usr/local/${args[0]}"
else
  echo "Invalid directory name"
  exit 1
fi
```

Temporary Files

Temporary files can pose security risks if not handled correctly. To mitigate risks such as race conditions and unauthorized access, use securely generated temporary directories or files:

```
temp_dir=$(mktemp -d)
file_path="$temp_dir/file.txt"
trap 'rm -rf "$temp_dir"' EXIT

# Continue script execution
# ...
```

The ‘mktemp -d‘ command creates a secure temporary directory, and the ‘trap‘ command ensures cleanup upon script exit.

Using Proper Permissions

Ensure scripts and related files have proper access permissions to prevent unauthorized modification or execution:

```
chmod 700 script.sh
chmod 600 sensitive_data.txt
```

Setting restrictive permissions with ‘chmod 700‘ and ‘chmod 600‘ ensures that only the owner has read, write, and execute permissions on scripts and sensitive data files, minimizing unauthorized access risks.

Chapter 10

Debugging and Testing Bash Scripts

This chapter focuses on debugging and testing Bash scripts. It covers the use of Bash debugging options, tracing script execution, and employing breakpoints and watchpoints. Additionally, it addresses common debugging pitfalls, using ShellCheck for testing, writing unit tests, and adopting Test Driven Development (TDD) practices. The chapter concludes with methods for automating tests and best practices for maintaining high-quality scripts.

10.1 Introduction to Debugging

Bash scripting, like any form of programming, is prone to errors and bugs that can lead to unintended behavior or program failures. Debugging is the systematic process of identifying, isolating, and fixing these errors. This section will introduce the fundamental concepts and tools necessary for debugging Bash scripts, aiming to build a strong foundation for more advanced topics discussed later in the chapter.

Errors Types in Bash Scripts

Errors in Bash scripts can broadly be categorized into three types:

- **Syntax Errors**: These occur when the script does not conform to the syntax rules of the Bash language.

- **Runtime Errors**: These occur during the execution of the script, often due to invalid operations or unmet conditions.
- **Logical Errors**: These are the most difficult to identify, as the script executes without errors but produces incorrect or unintended results.

Syntax Errors can be caught before execution using tools like bash -n. Runtime Errors often require dynamic analysis and careful examination of the script during execution. Logical Errors necessitate a deep understanding of the script's intended functionality and rigorous testing.

Debugging Basics

Effective debugging typically follows a structured approach:

- Reproduce the Error: Ensure that the error can be consistently reproduced. This step might involve simplifying the script or isolating the problematic code segments.
- Understand the Error Message: Bash provides error messages that give clues to the nature of the problem. Analyzing these messages is crucial to identifying the source.
- Trace the Execution: Investigate the flow of the script to understand where it diverges from the expected behavior.
- Modify and Test: Make incremental changes to the script and test repeatedly to observe the effect of each change on the script's behavior.

By following this methodical process, one can systematically address and resolve bugs in Bash scripts.

Using set for Debugging

Bash provides built-in options that facilitate debugging. The set command is particularly useful for this purpose. Key options include:

- -x: Print commands and their arguments as they are executed. This is known as execution tracing.
- -e: Exit immediately if a command exits with a non-zero status. This option is useful for identifying failures as soon as they occur.

- -u: Treat unset variables as an error when performing parameter expansion.
- -v: Print shell input lines as they are read.
- -n: Read commands but do not execute them; this syntax checking mode is invaluable for identifying syntax errors.

Example usage of these options is shown below:

```
#!/bin/bash

set -x # Enable execution tracing
set -e # Exit on errors

# Sample script with potential issues
echo "Starting script"
variable1="Hello"
echo $variable2 # This will cause an error due to an unset variable
echo ${variable2:-"Default"} # Correct usage with a default value

set +x # Disable execution tracing
set +e # Disable exit on errors
```

In the example, set -x enables tracing, printing each command before execution. When set -e is used, the script aborts immediately if any command exits with a non-zero status, facilitating error identification. Unused with syntactic coding, set -u and set -v can similarly aid debugging by stringent variable checking and input line printing, respectively.

Practical Debugging Tips

Effective debugging requires attention to detail and a systematic approach. Some tips to keep in mind include:

- Add Comments: Increase the use of comments to clarify the purpose and expected behavior of different sections within the script.
- Use Temporary Variables: Break complex expressions into simpler ones using temporary variables to isolate errors more effectively.
- Check External Resources: Ensure that external commands, files, and resources are present and accessible as expected by the script.
- Review Logs: Use logging mechanisms to record script execution details, which can be invaluable when diagnosing long-running or complex scripts.

By embedding these practices into the debugging routine, one can enhance the effectiveness and efficiency of resolving issues in Bash scripts.

Overall, debugging is an essential skill in scripting, necessitating a blend of methodical analysis and practical tools. Mastery of these introductory techniques lays the groundwork for more sophisticated debugging and testing methods, ensuring robust and reliable Bash scripts.

10.2 Using Bash Debugging Options

Bash provides several built-in options to facilitate the debugging process. These options allow for detailed introspection of the script's behavior, making it easier to identify and resolve issues. Here we will explore these options: set -x, set -v, and set -e, among others.

The set command in Bash is used to change the value of shell attributes and positional parameters or to display their values. By configuring certain options, we can modify the default behavior of the script execution, gaining deeper insights into the script's performance.

set -x enables a mode of the shell where all executed commands are printed to the terminal. This is extremely helpful for tracking command execution and diagnosing where the script might be failing. Here is a simple example:

```
#!/bin/bash
set -x
echo "This is a test"
variable="Hello World"
echo $variable
set +x
echo "Debugging ended"
```

Executing this script will yield:

```
+ echo 'This is a test'
This is a test
+ variable='Hello World'
+ echo Hello World
Hello World
+ set +x
+ echo 'Debugging ended'
Debugging ended
```

In this example, each command is prefixed with a + symbol, indicating its execution. The use of set +x disables this debugging mode, allowing the script to continue without command tracing.

set -v causes shell input lines to be printed as they are read. This can be critical when debugging more complex scripts or when dealing with malformed input. Consider the example:

```
#!/bin/bash
set -v
echo "This is a test"
variable="Hello World"
echo $variable
set +v
echo "Debugging ended"
```

The output produced will be:

```
#!/bin/bash
set -v
echo "This is a test"
This is a test
variable="Hello World"
echo $variable
Hello World
set +v
echo "Debugging ended"
Debugging ended
```

The output mirrors the commands and their execution, allowing for identification of syntax errors or logical errors in the script's flow. One can use both set -x and set -v in conjunction, providing both command and input tracing.

set -e instructs the script to exit immediately if any command exits with a non-zero status. This is particularly useful in preventing cascading failures where an error in one command can affect subsequent commands. For instance:

```
#!/bin/bash
set -e
echo "This is a test"
nonexistent_command
echo "This will not be printed"
```

In this scenario, the script will terminate upon encountering the nonexistent command, ensuring that no further execution occurs after the point of failure:

```
This is a test
./script.sh: line 4: nonexistent_command: command not found
```

Another useful debugging option is set -u, which treats unset variables as an error when performing parameter expansion. This can catch potential bugs where variables are assumed to be defined but are not. For example:

```
#!/bin/bash
set -u
```

```
echo "Variable value is: $variable"
```

Executing this script results in an error:

```
./script.sh: line 3: variable: unbound variable
```

This behavior emphasizes the importance of variable initialization and helps identify logical errors in conditional branching.

Lastly, the set -o pipefail option can be invaluable when working with pipelines. Normally, a pipeline's return status is that of the last command in the pipeline. With set -o pipefail, the pipeline will return the exit status of the first command that fails, which is crucial for accurately detecting and handling errors in complex scripts. Consider the following:

```
#!/bin/bash
set -o pipefail
echo "Testing pipefail"
false | true
echo "This will not be printed"
```

The false command will cause the pipeline to fail, and the subsequent commands will not execute:

```
Testing pipefail
```

By leveraging these Bash debugging options, scripts can be made more robust and easier to maintain. Integrating these options should be done thoughtfully, as excessive debugging output can become overwhelming. Instead, use these tools to pinpoint specific issues selectively, which aids in maintaining a clean and efficient debugging workflow.

10.3 Tracing Script Execution

Tracing script execution is a fundamental technique in debugging Bash scripts, allowing the developer to observe the step-by-step execution of the script. This section will delve into the methods of tracing, the significance of each technique, and how to apply them effectively in real-world scenarios.

Enabling Trace Mode

Bash provides a built-in mechanism for tracing script execution using the set built-in command with the -x option. When trace mode is enabled, each command and its arguments are printed to the standard error as they are executed.

To enable trace mode, insert the following command at the beginning of your script:

```
set -x
```

To disable trace mode, use the +x option:

```
set +x
```

Alternatively, trace mode can be enabled for the entire script execution by invoking the script with the -x option:

```
bash -x script.sh
```

Selective Tracing with Functions

Selective tracing can be implemented to trace only specific parts of the script. This is particularly useful for isolating problematic sections without cluttering the output with unnecessary information. Enabling and disabling trace mode around specific function calls achieves this:

```
trace_function() {
    set -x
    # Function code here
    set +x
}
```

Trace Output Analysis

Understanding the trace output is crucial for effective debugging. Each traced line is prefixed with a + sign, followed by the command and its arguments:

```
+ echo 'Start tracing'
Start tracing
+ ls -l
total 8
-rwxrwxr-x 1 user user  113 Sep 17 10:22 script.sh
```

Tracing with the PS4 Variable

The PS4 variable customizes the trace output format. By default, PS4 is set to +:

```
PS4='+ '
```

To enhance trace output readability, modify PS4 to include additional information, such as the script name and line number:

```
export PS4='+ $(basename ${BASH_SOURCE}):${LINENO}: '
```

Then, the trace output format incorporates the script name and line number:

```
+ script.sh:2: echo 'Start tracing'
Start tracing
+ script.sh:3: ls -l
total 8
-rwxrwxr-x 1 user user  113 Sep 17 10:22 script.sh
```

Debugging Complex Scripts

For complex scripts, tracing can produce extensive output. In such cases, direct the trace output to a file for further analysis:

```
bash -x script.sh > trace_output.txt 2>&1
```

After execution, the trace output is saved to trace_output.txt, which can then be inspected using any text editor.

Combining Tracing with trap

Combining tracing with the trap command adds another layer of robustness to debugging. The trap command executes a specified command when the script receives a signal. For example, to enable trace mode when a script encounters an error, use:

```
trap 'set -x' ERR
```

This enables trace mode when any command in the script returns a non-zero exit status, aiding in pinpointing the source of errors.

Practical Example

Consider a script that processes input files and performs a series of operations:

```
#!/bin/bash

process_file() {
    local file=$1
    echo "Processing $file"
    # Simulated processing steps
    grep "pattern" "$file"
    sort "$file" -o "$file.sorted"
    mv "$file.sorted" "$file"
}

main() {
    set -x # Enable trace mode
    for file in "$@"; do
        process_file "$file"
```

```
    done
    set +x # Disable trace mode
}

main "$@"
```

Execute the script with the test inputs:

```
./script.sh file1.txt file2.txt
```

The trace output includes each command executed by the script, providing insights into the script's behavior and facilitating the identification of issues.

Automated Testing Considerations

When integrating tracing into automated testing frameworks, ensure trace output is parsed effectively without overwhelming the test logs. Consider enabling trace mode conditionally based on an environment variable or command line option to control its verbosity during automated runs. For example:

```
#!/bin/bash

TRACE=${TRACE:-0}
[[ $TRACE -eq 1 ]] && set -x

# Rest of the script
```

To enable tracing, execute the script with TRACE=1:

```
TRACE=1 ./script.sh file1.txt file2.txt
```

Using the strategies outlined in this section enhances script debugging efficiency by providing a detailed, step-by-step account of script execution, enabling precise identification and rectification of errors.

10.4 Using breakpoints and watchpoints

Breakpoints and watchpoints are essential tools in the debugging process of Bash scripts. These mechanisms allow the script to pause execution at specific points or monitor the value changes of certain variables. Integral to effective debugging, they provide valuable insights that help identify and resolve issues efficiently.

To set a breakpoint in a Bash script, one can insert the read command at strategic locations within the script. This command pauses the script's execution and waits for user input, thus effectively serving as a manual breakpoint. Consider the following example of a Bash script:

```
#!/bin/bash

# Example script with breakpoints
variable1="Initial Value"
echo "Before breakpoint: variable1 is $variable1"
read -p "Press Enter to continue..." # Breakpoint

variable1="Changed Value"
echo "After breakpoint: variable1 is $variable1"
```

Upon execution, the script will halt at the read command, allowing the user to inspect the current state of the script's execution, such as the values of variables or the output of commands executed thus far. The script proceeds when the user presses Enter.

Watchpoints, on the other hand, monitor variables' values and trigger a breakpoint-like behavior when specific conditions involving these variables are met. Although Bash does not natively support watchpoints as more sophisticated debuggers (e.g., GDB for C/C++), crafty workarounds exploit the trap builtin command. trap allows the execution of a command when the script receives a signal, such as a variable assignment.

An innovative way to simulate watchpoints in Bash involves using trap with the DEBUG signal. This signal is triggered before every command executes within the script. The example below demonstrates a watchpoint that pauses execution when a variable exceeds a particular value:

```
#!/bin/bash

# Example script with watchpoint
variable_watched=0

# Function to set a watchpoint
watch_variable() {
  if (( variable_watched > 5 )); then
    echo "Watchpoint hit: variable_watched is greater than 5"
    read -p "Press Enter to continue..."
  fi
}

# Setting trap to call watch_variable function before executing each command
trap 'watch_variable' DEBUG

echo "Varying variable_watched from 0 to 10"

for (( i=0; i<=10; i++ )); do
  variable_watched=$i
  echo "Iteration $i: variable_watched is $variable_watched"
done
```

In this script, the trap command associates the watch_variable function with the DEBUG signal. As the for loop executes, the watch_variable function runs before each command. When variable_watched exceeds 5, the script pauses, allowing inspection and providing control over how to proceed.

Implementing breakpoints and watchpoints effectively requires thoughtful placement within the script. Key considerations include:

- Identifying critical sections of the script prone to errors or requiring close monitoring.
- Placing breakpoints before and after significant operations or command sequences to verify intermediate states.
- Using watchpoints to monitor variables whose values critically affect script behavior or outcomes.

Breakpoints and watchpoints significantly enhance debugging efficacy. However, over-reliance can clutter the script and disrupt normal execution flow. Employ them judiciously, removing or commenting out read commands and trap statements once their purpose has been fulfilled.

Continual practice with breakpoints and watchpoints will refine scripting skills, leading to more efficient problem-solving and robust script design. The knowledge gained from utilizing these tools will be invaluable in improving overall script quality and reliability.

10.5 Common Debugging Pitfalls

When debugging Bash scripts, it is essential to recognize and avoid common pitfalls that can hinder the debugging process and potentially lead to erroneous conclusions or prolonged debugging times. This section details these common pitfalls and provides strategies to avoid them, ensuring effective and efficient debugging.

One prevalent pitfall is neglecting to account for the environment in which the script runs. Environment variables, shell options, and inherited settings can profoundly impact script behavior. It is critical to ensure that the script's environment is consistent and meets the expected conditions. To diagnose environment-related issues, display and verify the state of important environment variables at relevant points using echo or declare -p.

Another frequent source of issues is improper handling of whitespace. Bash scripting is highly sensitive to whitespace, and unintentional spaces can alter the syntactical meaning of commands. Ensure that variable assignments and command substitutions do not contain extraneous whitespace. For instance, consider the difference between:

```
VAR=value # Correct
VAR = value # Incorrect
```

Implicit expansions can also be troublesome. In Bash, various types of expansions such as parameter expansion, command substitution, and arithmetic expansion can produce unintended results if not carefully managed. Using set -u can help catch unset variables which is a common source of bugs.

```
#!/bin/bash
set -u # Treat unset variables as errors

echo "Starting script"
echo "User is $USER" # This will cause an error if $USER is not set
```

Another common mistake is mishandling quotes, which can lead to strings or variable contents being interpreted wrongly. Consistently use double quotes around variable references to preserve their values and prevent word splitting. For instance:

```
VAR="Hello World"
echo $VAR # Incorrect: can cause word splitting
echo "$VAR" # Correct: preserves value with spaces
```

Command substitutions can mask errors, especially if they silently fail, leading to subtle bugs. To ensure visibility of errors within command substitutions, utilize the set -e option. This option causes the script to exit immediately if a command within a substitution fails:

```
#!/bin/bash
set -e

result=$(nonexistentcommand) # This will cause the script to exit
echo "Result is $result"
```

Misunderstanding the return status of commands and incorrect handling of exit codes can facilitate skipping over errors. Bash functions and external commands return status codes that should be carefully checked:

```
my_function() {
    return 1
}
```

```
my_function
if [ $? -ne 0 ]; then
    echo "my_function failed"
fi
```

Relying solely on echo statements for debugging can sometimes lead to insufficient insights into script behavior, particularly in complex scripts. Augment echo statements with tools like set -x and set -v for detailed tracing. This provides a comprehensive view of command execution and variable evaluation.

Ignoring error messages or not logging them appropriately is a serious mistake. Redirecting error messages to a log file and reviewing them helps catch errors early. Utilizing 2> redirection, logging frameworks, or dedicated logging functions can manage this effectively.

```
command_that_might_fail 2> error.log
```

Incorrectly evaluating conditions within loops and conditional statements is another debugging challenge. Ensure the correct logical operators (-eq, -ne, -lt, etc.) and glob constructs are used as intended:

```
if [ "$VAR" -eq "10" ]; then
    echo "VAR equals 10"
fi
```

Use parentheses for arithmetic evaluation and braces for command grouping to avoid precedence issues:

```
if (( VAR == 10 )); then
    echo "VAR equals 10"
fi

{ command1; command2; }
```

Omitting to test edge cases or failing to handle unexpected input can result in scripts that work under normal conditions but fail otherwise. Incorporating comprehensive error handling and input validation ensures robustness.

Finally, failing to use debugging tools like ShellCheck can lead to missed syntax errors and inefficiencies. ShellCheck analyzes scripts and provides suggestions for best practices, common errors, and security issues. integrating tools like ShellCheck into your development workflow significantly enhances script quality.

Avoiding these common pitfalls streamlines and enhances the debugging process, leading to more reliable and maintainable Bash scripts.

10.6 Testing with ShellCheck

ShellCheck is an open-source tool that provides static analysis for shell scripts. It is designed to quickly identify and correct errors in scripts, thereby improving their reliability and maintainability. This section explains how to install ShellCheck, use it to test Bash scripts, interpret its output, and integrate it into development workflows.

Installing ShellCheck

ShellCheck can be installed on various operating systems through different package managers. For a comprehensive installation guide, visit the official ShellCheck website. Below are the common installation commands for major platforms:

- **On Debian/Ubuntu:**

```
sudo apt-get install shellcheck
```

- **On Red Hat/Fedora:**

```
sudo dnf install ShellCheck
```

- **On macOS:**

```
brew install shellcheck
```

- **From source:**

```
git clone https://github.com/koalaman/shellcheck.git
cd shellcheck
cabal install
```

Basic Usage

To use ShellCheck, run the following command in the terminal, specifying the script file you want to test:

```
shellcheck script.sh
```

ShellCheck will analyze script.sh and output any issues it finds. Understanding how to interpret this output is crucial for effectively troubleshooting and correcting your script.

Interpreting ShellCheck Output

ShellCheck provides detailed outputs indicating the type of issue, the line number, and a suggested fix. Below is a sample output:

```
In script.sh line 3:
echo "Hello World
^-- SC1009: The mentioned here-string is empty (it does nothing).
```

In this example:

- In script.sh line 3: indicates where the issue is located.
- echo "Hello World shows the problematic code segment.
- ^– SC1009: The mentioned here-string is empty (it does nothing). provides the specific issue code and description.

Common ShellCheck Warnings and Errors

There are numerous warnings and errors that ShellCheck can identify. Here are some typical examples and their meanings:

- SC1009: The mentioned here-string is empty (it does nothing). - This warning indicates that a here-string is empty, which is often unintended.
- SC2006: Use $(...) notation instead of backticks. - This advises the use of $(...) for command substitution instead of backticks, enhancing readability and nesting.
- SC2086: Double quote to prevent globbing and word splitting. - This error suggests adding double quotes around variables to avoid unintentional splitting or globbing.

Configuring ShellCheck

ShellCheck allows configuration through command-line options and configuration files (e.g., .shellcheckrc). Common options include:

- -e CODE: Exclude certain checks. Useful for ignoring specific warnings.
- -s shell: Specify the shell type (sh, bash, dash, etc.).
- -f format: Select output format (gcc, json, tty, etc.).

```
shellcheck -e SC2086 -s bash script.sh
```

This example runs ShellCheck on script.sh, excluding warning SC2086 and specifying the shell type as Bash.

Integrating ShellCheck into Workflows

Integrating ShellCheck into your development process enhances script quality and consistency. Here are some methods to incorporate ShellCheck:

- **Editor Integration:** Many text editors (e.g., VS Code, Sublime Text) have ShellCheck plugins that automatically scan scripts on save.
- **Pre-commit Hooks:** Use Git hooks to run ShellCheck before committing changes. This ensures only compliant scripts enter the repository.
- **Continuous Integration (CI) Pipelines:** Integrate ShellCheck with CI tools (e.g., Jenkins, GitHub Actions) to automate script testing.

```
#!/bin/sh
# pre-commit hook for Git
shellcheck script.sh
if [ $? -ne 0 ]; then
    echo "ShellCheck failed, aborting commit."
    exit 1
fi
```

Ensure the hook script is executable and placed in the .git/hooks directory.

Adopting ShellCheck into your routines streamlines error detection and improves script performance and reliability, making your Bash scripting endeavors more efficient and effective.

10.7 Writing Unit Tests for Bash Scripts

Unit testing in Bash scripts involves creating small tests that check the functionality of individual parts of the script. The primary goal is to isolate and test each unit of the program to ensure it behaves as expected. Unlike traditional compiled languages, Bash scripting is interpretative and dynamic, meaning that testing can be approached in a similarly dynamic and flexible manner. To establish a solid foundation for unit testing Bash scripts, we employ tools like bats (Bash Automated Testing System).

Introduction to Bats

bats is a TAP-compliant testing framework for Bash. It offers a straightforward syntax to write tests and provides helpful output in case of test failures. To install bats, you can use a package manager like brew on macOS or apt-get on Debian-based systems.

```
# On macOS
brew install bats-core

# On Debian-based systems
sudo apt-get install bats
```

Creating and Running Tests

A bats test file typically has a .bats extension. Each test is a function whose name starts with the word test. bats collects and runs these functions, reporting the results.

Consider a simple Bash script, greet.sh, that prints a greeting message based on the input provided.

```
#!/bin/bash

greet() {
    local name=$1
    echo "Hello, $name!"
}

greet "$@"
```

We can create a test file for this script, greet_test.bats, to verify its functionality.

```
#!/usr/bin/env bats

@test "Greet with input" {
    run ./greet.sh Alice
    [ "$status" -eq 0 ]
    [ "$output" = "Hello, Alice!" ]
}
```

In the example above, the run command executes the greet.sh script with Alice as an argument. The status variable captures the exit status, and output contains the script's output. The tests verify that the script runs successfully and produces the correct output.

Handling Edge Cases

It is essential to test for various scenarios, including edge cases, to ensure robustness. For the greet.sh script, an edge case could be testing the behavior when no argument is provided.

```
#!/usr/bin/env bats

@test "Greet with no input" {
    run ./greet.sh
    [ "$status" -eq 0 ]
    [ "$output" = "Hello, !" ]
}
```

This test checks that the script runs without error even when no name is provided, and the output is as expected.

Testing for Failures

Testing for potential failures and erroneous inputs is crucial. Extending the greet.sh script to handle empty or null inputs can improve its robustness.

```
#!/bin/bash

greet() {
    if [ -z "$1" ]; then
        echo "Error: No name provided" >&2
        return 1
    fi
    local name=$1
    echo "Hello, $name!"
}

greet "$@"
```

Update the unit tests to handle and verify these cases:

```
#!/usr/bin/env bats

@test "Greet with input" {
    run ./greet.sh Alice
    [ "$status" -eq 0 ]
    [ "$output" = "Hello, Alice!" ]
}

@test "Greet with no input" {
    run ./greet.sh
    [ "$status" -eq 1 ]
    [ "$output" = "Error: No name provided" ]
}
```

Here, the script returns an error message and exits with a status of

1 if no name is provided. The tests ensure this behavior is correctly implemented.

Mocking External Commands

Mocking external commands is an effective way to isolate and test script components. Suppose the greet.sh script uses the date command to include the current date in the greeting.

```
#!/bin/bash

greet() {
    local name=$1
    local date=$(date '+%Y-%m-%d')
    echo "Hello, $name! Today is $date."
}

greet "$@"
```

Testing this script can be challenging since the date command's output varies. We can create a mock script to replace the date command within our tests.

```
#!/usr/bin/env bats

setup() {
    mkdir -p bin
    echo -e '#!/bin/bash\necho "2023-01-01"' > bin/date
    chmod +x bin/date
    export PATH=$PWD/bin:$PATH
}

teardown() {
    rm -rf bin
}

@test "Greet with date" {
    run ./greet.sh Alice
    [ "$status" -eq 0 ]
    [ "$output" = "Hello, Alice! Today is 2023-01-01." ]
}
```

In the above test file, the setup function creates a mock date command that always returns 2023-01-01. The teardown function cleans up after the tests. This ensures consistency in the test output.

Unit testing for Bash scripts with bats significantly enhances script reliability by ensuring individual script segments function correctly under various scenarios. This practice helps identify errors early and facilitates easier debugging and maintenance of complex scripts.

10.8 Test Driven Development (TDD) in Bash

Test Driven Development (TDD) is a software development approach that relies on the repetition of a very short development cycle. The developer writes an initially failing automated test case that defines a desired improvement or new function, then produces the minimum amount of code to pass that test, and finally refactors the new code to acceptable standards. This section elucidates the application of TDD in Bash scripting.

Writing a Test First

In TDD, we start by writing a test for a specific function or module before writing the actual implementation code. This ensures that the requirements are clear and validates functionality as development proceeds. For Bash scripts, we can leverage the bats (Bash Automated Testing System) framework to write and run test cases. Ensure that bats is installed on your system before proceeding.

Consider we need a function greet that takes a name as an argument and echoes a greeting.

First, create a test file greet_test.bats:

```
#!/usr/bin/env bats

@test "greet returns a greeting for the given name" {
  run ./greet.sh "Alice"
  [ "$status" -eq 0 ]
  [ "$output" = "Hello, Alice!" ]
}
```

In this test case:

- The @test annotation marks the beginning of a test named "greet returns a greeting for the given name".
- The run command executes the greet.sh script with "Alice" as an argument.
- The ["$status" -eq 0] line checks that the script exits with status 0, indicating success.
- The ["$output" = "Hello, Alice!"] line verifies that the script's output matches the expected greeting.

Running the Test

Before writing the greet.sh script, run the test:

```
$ bats greet_test.bats
```

Expected output:

```
  greet returns a greeting for the given name

1 test, 0 failures
```

Since we haven't implemented greet.sh, the test will fail initially. Now, we write the minimal code required to pass the test.

Create greet.sh:

```
#!/bin/bash

greet() {
  local name="$1"
  echo "Hello, $name!"
}

greet "$@"
```

With the script implemented, run the test again:

```
$ bats greet_test.bats
```

Expected output:

```
  greet returns a greeting for the given name

1 test, 0 failures
```

The test should now pass, confirming that the function greet behaves as expected.

Refactoring

With the test passing, we can refactor the code to improve readability or maintainability without altering its functionality. The test case provides a safety net ensuring that changes do not inadvertently break existing behavior.

For example, we might refactor greet.sh to:

```
#!/bin/bash

greet() {
  local name="${1:-World}"
  echo "Hello, $name!"
}

greet "$@"
```

This refactored version defaults to greeting "World" when no name is provided. Rerun the test to ensure it still passes:

```
$ bats greet_test.bats
```

Adding More Tests

In TDD, new functionalities should be validated by new tests. Adding a default case for when no name is provided.

Update greet_test.bats:

```
#!/usr/bin/env bats

@test "greet returns a greeting for the given name" {
  run ./greet.sh "Alice"
  [ "$status" -eq 0 ]
  [ "$output" = "Hello, Alice!" ]
}

@test "greet returns a default greeting when no name is given" {
  run ./greet.sh
  [ "$status" -eq 0 ]
  [ "$output" = "Hello, World!" ]
}
```

Run the expanded test suite:

```
$ bats greet_test.bats
```

Expected output:

```
  greet returns a greeting for the given name
  greet returns a default greeting when no name is given

2 tests, 0 failures
```

Incorporating TDD in Bash scripting fosters a disciplined approach to development, enhances code quality, and ensures reliable, maintainable scripts are produced.

Benefits and Challenges

- **Immediate Feedback:** Tests provide instant feedback on code changes, facilitating rapid iteration.
- **Code Coverage:** Writing tests first ensures all functionalities are validated.
- **Design Improvement:** Forces consideration of interface and design before implementation.
- **Maintenance Overhead:** Writing and maintaining tests requires effort, initially increasing development time.
- **Applicable Tests:** Ensuring test cases are meaningful and maintain their relevance as the code evolves is crucial.

Testing and debugging comprise critical components in the lifecycle of Bash scripting, and adopting TDD practices can significantly enhance robustness and reliability.

10.9 Automating Tests

Automating tests in Bash scripting plays a vital role in ensuring that scripts remain reliable and maintainable over time. By integrating automated tests into the development workflow, developers can promptly detect regressions or bugs introduced by changes. Automated testing provides a consistent and repeatable process for verifying script functionality, which is essential for maintaining code quality, especially in complex or rapidly evolving projects.

1. Overview of Automated Testing Tools

Several tools and frameworks are available for automating tests in Bash scripts:

- bats: Bash Automated Testing System, or Bats, is a TAP-compliant testing framework for Bash. It allows writing test cases in a straightforward and readable format.
- shUnit2: A unit test framework for shell scripts. It is similar to frameworks like JUnit and can be used to write unit tests in a manner suited for shell scripts.
- Custom scripts: Writing custom Bash scripts for testing purposes can be advantageous, especially for simple projects, by providing greater control and flexibility.

2. Using bats for Automated Testing

Installing and Setting Up bats:

To install Bats, you can use a package manager like Homebrew on macOS or download the source from the GibHub repository:

```
# Using Homebrew (macOS)
brew install bats-core

# Cloning from GitHub and installing
git clone https://github.com/bats-core/bats-core.git
cd bats-core
sudo ./install.sh /usr/local
```

Creating Test Files with bats:

Bats test files have a .bats extension and comprise test cases written as Bash functions. Each test case should be prefixed with the keyword test followed by a description.

Example:

```
#!/usr/bin/env bats

@test "test example script returns correct output" {
  result="$(./example_script.sh)"
  [ "$result" = "expected output" ]
}
```

Executing bats Tests:

To run the tests, simply invoke the bats command followed by the test file or directory containing test files:

```
bats example_tests.bats
```

```
  test example script returns correct output

1 test, 0 failures
```

3. Example Test Script with Assertions

Assertions are used to verify that the output or behavior of the script under test is as expected. Bats provides several assertion functions such as assert_equal, assert_not_equal, assert_true, and assert_false.

Example:

```
#!/usr/bin/env bats

load './bats-support/load'
load './bats-assert/load'

@test "check if file exists" {
  run ./file_check.sh
  assert_true [ -f "testfile.txt" ]
}

@test "output should match expected" {
  run ./output_check.sh
  assert_output "hello world"
}
```

4. Automating Tests with Continuous Integration (CI)

Integrating automated tests into a Continuous Integration pipeline ensures that tests are executed each time changes are pushed to the repository. This practice helps in instantaneously identifying issues introduced by new code modifications.

Example: Setting Up a GitHub Actions Workflow

A GitHub Actions workflow can be created by adding a .github/workflows/test.yml file to the repository:

```
name: CI

on:
  push:
    branches:
      - main
  pull_request:
    branches:
      - main

jobs:
  test:
    runs-on: ubuntu-latest

    steps:
    - uses: actions/checkout@v2
    - name: Set up Bats
      run: |
        sudo apt-get update
        sudo apt-get install -y bats
    - name: Run tests
      run: bats tests/
```

5. Benefits of Automating Tests

Automating tests in Bash scripts offers multiple benefits:

- Consistency: Automated tests are executed in the same manner every time, reducing the risk of human error.
- Efficiency: Automated tests can be run frequently and simultaneously, ensuring that issues are detected early and consistently.
- Scalability: As projects grow, the number of tests can scale accordingly without significant manual effort.
- Documentation: Automated tests serve as documentation that specifies the intended behavior of scripts, providing clarity to future contributors.

Such practices ensure robust and maintainable Bash scripts, ready to handle real-world scenarios with reliability.

10.10 Best Practices for Debugging and Testing

Effective debugging and testing of Bash scripts are critical for ensuring the quality and reliability of your code. This section presents a comprehensive guide to the best practices for debugging and testing Bash scripts, focusing on methodical approaches, usage of available tools, and adherence to scripting standards.

One fundamental principle in debugging and testing scripts is **maintaining code readability and documentation**. Clear and concise comments in the script help both the original developer and others who may need to debug the code later. Use the echo command to print out values of variables and positions in the script to understand its flow and state.

```
# Example of adding debug prints
count=0
echo "Initial count: $count"
while [[ $count -lt 10 ]]; do
  echo "Current count: $count"
  ((count++))
done
echo "Final count: $count"
```

Encapsulate repetitive tasks into functions to enhance modularity and make scripts more manageable. This practice simplifies testing as functions can be tested independently.

```
function increment_count {
  local count=$1
  echo $((count + 1))
}

count=0
while [[ $count -lt 10 ]]; do
  count=$(increment_count $count)
  echo "Count after increment: $count"
done
```

Using strict mode in Bash scripts is another best practice. By setting set -euo pipefail, you can enforce more stringent error checking hence reducing the chances of unnoticed errors.

```
#!/bin/bash
set -euo pipefail

echo "Enter a number: "
read number
if [[ -z "$number" ]]; then
  echo "No input provided"
  exit 1
```

```
fi
echo "You entered: $number"
```

Effective use of debugging options such as set -x can provide a clearer view of script execution by printing each command before executing it. However, it's advisable to use it selectively to avoid cluttering the output, especially in large scripts.

```
#!/bin/bash
set -x
count=0
while [[ $count -lt 5 ]]; do
  ((count++))
  echo "Count: $count"
done
set +x
```

For **testing scripts systematically**, integrate tools like **ShellCheck**, which helps identify syntax and semantic issues in scripts. ShellCheck outputs are highly informative, providing suggestions for improving script quality.

```
$ shellcheck myscript.sh

In myscript.sh line 5:
if [ $count == 5 ]; then
       ^-- SC1073: Couldn't parse this test expression.
       ^-- SC2086: Double quote to prevent globbing and word splitting.
```

Automate the running of these checks by incorporating ShellCheck in Continuous Integration (CI) pipelines. By doing so, you ensure code quality remains high through consistent, automated evaluation.

Unit testing frameworks such as Bats (Bash Automated Testing System) offer structured testing methodologies for Bash scripts. Writing unit tests for individual functions ensures that each piece of functionality is verified against expected behaviors.

```
# Test file for increment_count function using Bats
@test "increment_count increments the count by 1" {
  result=$(increment_count 3)
  [ "$result" -eq 4 ]
}
```

When utilizing TDD practices, write your unit tests before implementing the function. This can drive development towards fulfilling the specified requirements early in the coding process, reducing the incidences of overlooked errors and slip-ups.

Lastly, adopt **version control** effectively. Keep track of different versions of your scripts using systems like Git. Commit often with clear, concise messages. Version control not only provides a historical trail of changes but also facilitates collaborative debugging and testing.

Implementing these best practices will fortify the robustness of your Bash scripts, leading to code that is both maintainable and reliable. An emphasis on readability, modularity, rigorous error checking, and systematic testing will contribute greatly to achieving high-quality script outcomes.

Made in United States
North Haven, CT
03 November 2026

21729485R00159